Presented To:

_____

_____

From:

_____

_____

Date:

_____

In the Garden
with God

Honor Books
Tulsa, Oklahoma

In the Garden with God
ISBN 1-56292-638-1
Copyright 2000 © by Honor Books
P.O. Box 55388
Tulsa, Oklahoma 74155

Manuscript written, compiled, and edited by Robert J. Exley, Rebecca Barlow
Jordan, Patti M. Hummel, Pauline M. Cramer, Gayle S. Edwards, and Marla M.
Patterson.

Printed in the United States of America. All rights reserved under International
Copyright Law. Contents and/or cover may not be reproduced in whole or in
part in any form without the express written consent of the Publisher.

In the Garden with God

Saved by the Weeds

Let both grow together until the harvest.
—Matthew 13:30

Farming, like other high-risk occupations, requires a great deal of faith, dependence, and trust in God's timing and goodness.

One year a potato farmer encountered some problems due to hot weather. Because potatoes are a very temperamental crop and must be in the ground a certain period of time the farmer was concerned that the planting be done on time.

The weather broke, however, and he planted the potatoes only five days late. As the cultivation program began, everything looked good except for two plots where weeds began to grow out of control two weeks before the harvest. It was too late to destroy the weeds. The farmer had to let them keep growing.

Saved by the Weeds

Another more severe problem emerged when a truck strike interfered with the targeted harvest date. The farmer knew that leaving his potatoes too long in the Arizona summer heat would destroy the crop. In the meantime, the "carpet weeds" continued to flourish and provided an almost blanket-like protection over the potatoes, while taller weeds gave additional shade. Later as the harvesters examined the fields, they discovered that wherever the weeds had grown up, there was no spoilage of potatoes. In weed-free areas, the potatoes were ruined because of the heat. The weeds saved his crops. He had only 5 percent spoilage.

God often uses seemingly adverse circumstances to shield and shade us from "spoilage" in our lives. The very "weeds" we chafe about—petty irritations, chronic interruptions, "irregular" people—are often the means He uses to enhance our ultimate growth and develop a harvest of godly character in us.

Never Give Up

Let us not grow become weary in doing good, for at the
proper time we will reap a harvest if we do not give up.
—*Galatians 6:9*

Again, the young teacher read the note attached
to the fresh green ivy.

"Because of the seeds you planted, we will one day
grow into beautiful plants like this one. We appreciate
all you've done for us. Thank you for investing time in
our lives."

A smile widened the teacher's face as grateful tears
trickled down her cheeks. Like the one leper who
expressed gratitude to Jesus for healing him, the girls
she had taught remembered to say thanks to their
Sunday School teacher. The ivy plant represented a
gift of love.

For months the teacher faithfully watered that
growing plant. Each time she looked at it, she

remembered those special teenagers and was encouraged to continue teaching.

But after a year, something happened. The leaves began to turn yellow and drop—all but one. She started to discard the ivy, but decided to keep watering and fertilizing it. One day as she walked through the kitchen, the teacher noticed a new shoot on the plant. A few days later, another leaf appeared, and then another. Within a few months, the ivy was well on its way to becoming a healthy plant again.

Henry Drummond says, "Do not think that nothing is happening because you do not see yourself grow, or hear the whir of the machinery. All great things grow noiselessly."

Few joys exceed the blessings of faithfully investing time and love into the lives of others. Never, never give up on those plants!

Clubfoot

There was given to me a thorn in the flesh.
—2 Corinthians 12:7 KJV

Phillip Carey, an orphan and the main character in the novel *Of Human Bondage*,[1] was born with what was once called a "clubfoot." Because of his deformity, his school classmates often made fun of him and excluded him from their boyhood games.

In one poignant scene, young Phillip is convinced that if he prays hard enough, God will heal his foot. He daydreams for hours about the reaction of his classmates when he returns to school with a new foot: he sees himself outrunning the swiftest boy in his class and takes great pleasure in the shocked amazement of his former tormentors. At last he goes to sleep knowing that when he awakes in the morning, his foot will be whole.

But the next day brings no change. He is still a clubfoot.

Although just one of many disappointments for young Phillip, this proves to be a pivotal point in his learning to cope with the harsh realities of his life. Drawing upon an inner strength he did not know he had, he found that his clubfoot would not determine his destiny. But how he responded to it would make all the difference in his life. If he viewed it as a crippling deformity, he would live a limited life. Instead, he began to see his handicap as nothing more than an obstacle to be overcome, and it did not hold him back.

Life is filled with grand opportunities cleverly camouflaged as devastating disappointments. For Phillip Carey, it was a clubfoot. For the Apostle Paul, it was a thorn in the flesh. Whatever it is in your life, don't despair. With God's help, you too can turn your scars into stars, your handicaps into strengths.

Believe in Me

*And the Lord make you to increase and abound
in love one toward another, and toward all men.*
—*I Thessalonians 3:12 KJV*

Cynthia was amazed and grateful for what she was seeing. Ms. Nelson, a fifth grade teacher at the private school where Cynthia worked, was quietly greeting each child and their parents at the door of her classroom. Ms. Nelson spoke with pride to each parent of the work of his or her child. She took time to mention the child by name and to point out something on that child's work that was particularly noteworthy. As a result, both the parent and the child glowed with satisfaction.

This was not a special event—it was the morning of a normal school day, and Ms. Nelson made it a habit to be at the door every morning.

As Cynthia stepped into her own office, she was struck by the impact of Ms. Nelson's genuine comments and actions. Cynthia couldn't help but think of a gardener fussing over the flowers and plants of the garden—eager to provide the right nourishment and attention so that each plant grows strong and healthy.

Later that afternoon, Cynthia asked her fifth-grade son John how he liked being in Ms. Nelson's class. John responded, "I like it a lot. She is a really neat teacher because you always know that she believes in you. Even when you don't get everything right, she still believes in you."

What a gift—the ability to believe in others and communicate it to them daily, just as our Lord loves and believes in us without fail. We can all learn to pass this gift on to those we care about.

Make Me a Channel of Blessing

And since we have gifts that differ according to the grace given to us, let each exercise them accordingly.
—Romans 12:6 NASB

Can you imagine a professional football tackle pitching for a major league baseball game? He might be able to throw the ball with speed because he is strong and in great physical condition, but he won't have a great knuckle ball or a split finger ball that just makes it over the inside corner of the plate for a strike. He isn't equipped to play that position in that setting.

While all athletes go through extensive training to strengthen their God-given talents, each player actually is a specialist in his or her sport of choice. There are rare occasions where an athlete can change from one sport to another and still play well. But even that athlete will function better in one particular sport, playing one particular position.

So, too, are our spiritual gifts. Each of us has talents, and God has asked us to be channels of blessing to others. We may be able to do many things—even do them well—but we will find the greatest fulfillment and success when we use our gifts the way God intended they be used.

Being prepared for the work God has called us to do begins with knowing what our gifts are, and then surrendering our gifts totally to Him. Knowing what we have to offer to our family, friends, and community helps us discover our unique place in God's garden.

Channels only, blessed Master,
But with all Thy wondrous power
Flowing thro' us, Thou canst use us
Ev-'ry day and ev-'ry hour.[2]

Clinging Vines

*I am the vine, you are the branches; he who abides
in Me, and I in him, he bears much fruit;
for apart from Me you can do nothing.*
—John 15:5 NASB

Scuppernong vines are parasites that grow up
the trunks of and cling to healthy, firmly rooted trees
in the southern United States. This walnut sized, dark
skinned wild grape is used to make jams and jellies
and some Southerners use the hull skins for cobbler
pies. The fruit produced by these vines has served as
an inexpensive treat to poor families in the South for
many years. In recent years scuppernongs have
become more popular and can be purchased at stores
all over the South.

As beautiful, diverse, and tasty as the scuppernong
is, it cannot survive on its own. It needs the life
support of well-established trees to cling to and draw
its nourishment from. Should the scuppernong vine

be pulled away from its host tree, it will dry up and stop producing fruit.

Like the scuppernong, we cannot survive without total dependency on God. Without Him, we have no true life source, no lifeline, no nourishment, and we cannot produce good fruit.

We can, however, learn to cling to the Lord by surrendering ourselves to Him. We can draw nourishment through Bible study, prayer, worship, service, and heartfelt obedience. Like the scuppernong, clinging to our Source will help us grow healthy and produce much good fruit.

The Olive Press

He went away again a second time and
prayed, saying, "My Father, if this cannot
pass away until I drink it, Thy will be done."
—Matthew 26:42 NASB

In Jerusalem one can stand in the Garden of
Gethsemane on the Mount of Olives and look across
the Kedron Valley to the Eastern Gate where Scriptures
say Jesus will return one day. There in the garden, one
of the olive trees is thought to be more than 2000 years
old. Perhaps it is the same one Jesus knelt beneath
when He agonized in prayer prior to the crucifixion.

The Israelites were familiar with the procedure of
making oil from the olives through a process of
pressing that took about three days. Olive oil became
a staple used for food and cooking. To this day, virgin
olive oil is much favored with gourmet cooks. In
biblical times, olive oil was burned in lamps as a

source of light. It was used in preservation, anointing, and healing. There is much spiritual significance associated with olive oil.

Perhaps it is no wonder that Christ knelt beneath an olive tree as He chose the path of the cross. When we follow Him we reflect His love, we are a good seasoning for the world, and we are lights in the darkness. When we place our trust in Him we are preserved until He comes again.

Today the Garden of Gethsemane is a favorite spot for visitors from around the globe. For each person, regardless of race or religion or background, the olive trees stand as constant reminders of God's grace and redeeming love.

Basket of Love

They will still yield fruit in old age;
they shall be full of sap and very green.
—Psalm 92:14 NASB

*E*very Thursday Jean, a senior citizen, hustled off
to visit the people on her list. Some resided in nursing
homes; others were lonely at home. Thankful she
could still drive, Jean filled a wicker basket with
bananas or flowers and sometimes included a cassette
tape of her church's Sunday service. Most of all, she
packed her basket with lots of love and concern for
others tucked in.

Jean often sat at the bedside of one feeble lady.
Although the woman did not respond, Jean treated her
tenderly as though she heard and understood every
word. Jean chatted about current happenings, read
Scripture, prayed, then kissed her goodbye at the end
of the visit and said, "I'll see you next week."

As Jean's friends began to pass away, she felt lonesome for them, but she never stopped serving the Lord. She just found new friends and kept sharing God's love until He called her home.

Like a sturdy basket used for a variety of practical needs, Jean filled her heart and life with love for others. With time and heavy use, baskets may wear out, but God continues to use His children to help others as long as we are willing to carry around His love. Whether we minister to others through prayer, meeting physical needs, sending cards, or just a telephone call, we can still serve.

Jean didn't just believe in God; she lived her faith by sharing her basket of God's love with all those around her.

Soul Hunger

*And the city has no need of the sun nor of the moon to
give light to it, for the splendor and radiance (glory)
of God illuminate it, and the Lamb is its lamp.*
—Revelation 21:23 AMP

Despite endless cloudy days this spring, the
columbines still managed to bloom. Blue, scarlet, and
gold bell-shaped flowers with delicate dangling spurs
towered over lacy foliage. They danced gracefully in
the breeze, their bright colors attracting
hummingbirds. Yet, without God's sun, they didn't
seem as radiant as in previous springs.

It is the same with humans. Although we follow
our genetic codes and grow into healthy people
physically, we have no radiance without the Son of
God. The windows of our souls appear cloudy, and
God's love cannot shine through us.

Just as columbines hunger for the sun's warm rays,
our souls hunger for the loving presence of Jesus.

Unlike the columbines, however, we can find the Son even on cloudy days of despair.

We can take action to find the Son by simply reading or listening to His Word and obeying it. We can meet Him in a flower garden with each stem and blossom appearing like a signpost to His presence. We hear His praises being sung by the rustle of leaves held like the trees' uplifted hands.

Getting to know Him in a personal way enlightens our souls. His radiance fills our hearts and enlivens our spirits with hope for eternal life with Him in heaven.

In heaven, the sun will not be needed because God Himself will be our light. Perhaps Heaven's columbines will always dance with radiance from the glow of God's glory.

Don't Blame the Lettuce!

Now he who plants and he who waters are one; but each
will receive his own reward according to his own labor.
—*1 Corinthians 3:8 NASB*

One evening, several college students spread Limburger cheese on the upper lip of a sleeping fraternity brother.

Upon awakening the young man sniffed, looked around, and said, "This room stinks!"

He then walked into the hall and said, "This hall stinks!"

Leaving the dormitory he exclaimed, "The whole world stinks!"[3]

How long do you think it took for that sleepy student to discover the problem was right under his own nose?

It is easy, and maybe even our nature, to find fault with the outside world while remaining blind to the ways we contribute to the problem. Are there times when *we're* the problem?

> *When you plant lettuce, if it does not grow well,*
> *you don't blame the lettuce. You look for reasons it*
> *is not doing well. It may need fertilizer, or more*
> *water, or less sun. You never blame the lettuce. Yet*
> *if we have problems with our friends or our*
> *family, we blame the other person. But if we know*
> *how to take care of them, they will grow well, like*
> *the lettuce. Blaming has no positive effect at all,*
> *nor does trying to persuade using reason and*
> *argument. That is my experience.*

In the garden of our relationships, it is our job as caretakers to seek the most nurturing climate and soil. We must uproot the weeds of negativity and self-righteousness and protect the tender plants from the heat of jealousy and harsh wind of anger. When we apply God's love and care to our dealings with the important people in our lives, our relationships will most certainly grow and flourish.

The Celebrity Garden

*I am a rose of Sharon. . . . Like a lily among
thorns is my darling among the maidens.*
—Song of Songs 2:1-2

Sherry had finally cleaned a spot in her back
yard for a rose garden—her dream for many years. As
she thumbed through a rose catalog, she sighed at the
magnitude of her choices. *Just like a Christmas wish list,*
she thought. *Which ones should I pick? A white John F.
Kennedy, a large, pink Peggy Lee, a red Mr. Lincoln, the
delicate Queen Elizabeth rose?*

Sherry closed her eyes as if in deep thought.
Suddenly, she had an idea, *I'll plant my own celebrity
garden.*

The next day Sherry hurried to her local nursery
and bought a dozen roses—all colors and sizes. She
worked hard that week, carefully planting each rose.
Finally, her task was done and she decided to throw a

party and invite all her friends to help her celebrate her celebrity rose garden.

Imagine their surprise when her friends watched Sherry unveil the celebrity names she had placed on each rose. One by one, they read their own names beside the flowers. The celebrities in Sherry's garden were none other than her friends. But in the middle of the fragrant bouquet, one rose still remained a mystery.

She unveiled the label which read, "Rose of Sharon." "This One is the love of my life, and everything else centers around Him."

A thousand "celebrities" cry out for our time and attention. Relationships, like a healthy garden, need ample doses of love and affirmation. When Christ is at the center of our affection, all other loves will fall in place.

In the garden of your life, who are your celebrities?

Spontaneous Love Bouquets

*Do not let your left hand know what your right hand is doing,
so that your giving may be in secret. Then your Father,
who sees what is done in secret, will reward you.*
—*Matthew 6: 3-4*

Melanie read the suggestions carefully. "Place contrasting colors together, like peach with blue. Or try red, white, and blue, for a bright, patriotic bed. If you prefer, naturalize your bulbs, incorporating them into your yard's natural habitat. This works particularly well if you live in a wooded, grassy area."

She grabbed her gardener's tools and set to work, planting some in circles and others in rows. Melanie reserved a handful of varied size bulbs, and like a mother hiding Easter eggs for her expectant child, she tossed bulbs randomly on the grass. Wherever they landed, Melanie carved a hole and dropped them in the ground.

Weeks passed and Melanie forgot about the bulbs—including their secret hiding places. One early spring day, Melanie walked out in her back yard and saw green shoots poking through the earth. In the next few weeks, her yard looked like a magical wonderland. As she strolled through the green terrain, she realized the most fun part was seeing the bulbs pop up among the natural setting—beside trees, in the middle of a grassy slope, or tucked away in a corner. Nature had worked its magic and rewarded Melanie's long-forgotten efforts with a harvest of beautiful flowers.

Christ-like deeds are like the bulbs in Melanie's garden. Some we plant in deliberate, orderly fashion. Others, because of the God-nature planted within us, spill out from our lives naturally like spontaneous love gifts to those around us. These colorful bouquets spring up in the most unexpected places, a true "God-thing," blessing us—and others—in a most beautiful way.

Taste the Honey

Increasing in the knowledge of God.
—Colossians 1:10 KJV

It was nearly eleven o'clock on a Saturday evening when they met at a local bookstore and café for coffee and conversation. The store was busy, filled with people reading, drinking coffee and cappuccinos, and sharing time with each other. Bob commented to his brother that the combination of sweets and learning brought to mind something he had read recently.

"Are you familiar with the work *Our Father Abraham?*" he asked. "Well, in one section, the author relates how the Jewish rabbis used honey in a most unusual way on the first day of school to emphasize the importance of learning divine truth."

"The young child was shown a slate which had written on it the letters of the alphabet, two verses of Scripture, and one other sentence. 'The Law will be my calling.' The teacher next read these words to the child, and the child repeated them back. Then his slate was coated with honey, which he promptly licked off, being reminded of Ezekiel, who said after eating the scroll, 'I ate it, and it tasted as sweet as honey in my mouth' (Ezekiel 3:3). After this ceremony, the child was given sweet cakes to eat with Bible verses from the Law written on them."[4]

After a moment of silence, Richard looked up at Bob and said, "We could learn much from that young Jewish boy with his honey and his slate. Whatever else we do each day, we can enjoy the sweetness of learning and reading the Word with eagerness. That's how we grow in grace and understanding."

Cats Become Dogs?

Brethren, be not children in understanding.
—I Corinthians 14:20 KJV

It had been years since the four siblings had been together, and the air was filled with laughter as they regaled their families with stories from their childhood. The three older brothers told story after story of the trials and tribulations of having three boys in one bedroom. They also told of the many practical jokes they played on one another and of the numerous fights they had had as kids. But no one could top Sherry's story of being the "baby-sister."

"You know, guys," she said during a momentary lull in the conversation, "I used to think that all cats would one day turn into dogs and that all people are born a girl and would turn into a boy. In fact, I used to wonder when I would become a boy just like you guys."

Cats Become Dogs?

"Thank goodness that didn't happen," she firmly stated.

When she was just a child, Sherry's concept made perfect sense. She had three older brothers and no sisters, so naturally she assumed she would one day become a boy, too. Of course, as she grew old enough to understand things better, this idea slipped away to become just a fond memory.

While physical growth and maturation occur independent of our control, how many times do we remain "children in our understanding" because we simply choose not to exercise our thinking abilities or because the issues we must face are just too uncomfortable? Yet we can seek God's wisdom and direction so that we might grow in our understanding of His desires for us.

Are you willing to accept that challenge today?

Grow Up!

And he will be like a tree firmly planted by
streams of water, which yields its fruit in its season.
—Psalm 1:3 NASB

"Grow up!" is a taunt often used by teenagers to their peers who, for whatever reason, aren't acting as mature as they should at the moment. The command is given with the attitude that the other person can simply make a choice to immediately grow up.

Commanding a friend to "grow up" doesn't do any more good than it would to tell a tree to "grow up." There is a process that must take place, and that process takes time. Every living thing requires certain elements in order to grow—good soil, the appropriate amounts of sunshine and water, and plenty of time.

People, like trees, need a good start in order to be rooted securely. Young saplings can't mature into beautiful and tall shade trees without the right mixture of sun, water, rich soil, and space. As long as a tree is living, it never stops growing and never outgrows its need for nourishment. Most importantly, this process takes time—and lots of it.

In God's perfect timing, we will indeed "grow up." Like a baby taking the first steps, so we must be willing to let nature takes its course. The growth process is a long one, and it never really is complete. Flourishing trees don't strain to grow. They merely follow the natural process God planted in them. And healthy trees don't decide to just ignore the nourishment of sun, rain, and soil. Instead, they continually draw life from these things.

No matter what our "season" of life, growing up is a continuous process—and it all happens in God's time.

Yule Log

Thy name, O Lord, is everlasting, Thy remembrance,
O Lord, throughout all generations.
—Psalm 135:13 NASB

It took place around the second week of December every year. Mother would open her cedar chest and gingerly begin to sort through her most prized material possessions. She took such care as she reached inside and one by one removed items that held great meaning to her. Bubble lights, treasured Christmas tree, ornaments, tinsel, and many things shiny and fragrant renewed the season year after year.

One special item was placed on the mantel, transforming the home. It was a Yule Log, covered in artificial hyssop and man-made holly berries. It had a place in the center for a candle. A bright red satin ribbon was attached with a metal staple on the end to enhance its beauty.

Yule Log

Each year, the family had a tradition of discussing the Yule Log and remembering what each part of the decoration meant. The log signified a celebration, the birth of Christ. Hyssop, a fragrant herb, was used in ancient Hebrew sacrifices. The lovely red satin ribbon signified the blood of Christ that was shed for our sins. The holly berries represented growth, a bountiful supply. And the candle glowed as a loving reminder that Christ is the Light of the World.

Sometimes in the ordinary, sometimes in our traditions, sometimes in our celebrations, we can find the foundation of our faith. Here, a plain log, a few faded green leaves, some old berries, and a tattered ribbon tell the ageless story of God's infinite love.

Just Like Daddy

*And God created man in His own image, in the image of
God He created him; male and female He created them.*
—Genesis 1:27 NASB

The snow-covered peaks, fragrant evergreens,
and a rustic lodge combined to create a picture-perfect
postcard scene. Inside the adjacent condo, a
grandmother kept her five-month-old granddaughter
while the baby's parents took their turn skiing. After
Emily had her nap, bottle, and playtime, the
grandmother then zipped her into a feather-soft blue
bunting and carried her toward the lobby to await the
family's return.

Other guests and hotel workers began smiling
when they saw the baby. They approached her, talked
baby talk, and reached out to touch her chubby
cheeks. Emily's flawless skin and innocent blue eyes
captured everyone's attention. Big strong athletic skiers
paused to coo with Emily. Seasoned seniors who had

seen decades of history delighted in Emily's innocence. Weary travelers paused from their hectic schedules to smile and "talk" with Emily.

The shuttle bus soon pulled into the driveway. As Emily's parents entered the lobby, she recognized them and squealed with delight. A lady sitting nearby commented, "Why, Little Girl, you look just like your daddy!" Everyone chuckled because it was true. Although only a little face peered from the bunting, anyone—even a stranger—could see the strong resemblance.

When people see us, does our joy overflow to them? Do we delight the hearts of people who cross our paths? Does the image of our Heavenly Daddy reflect in the light of our eyes? Will people recognize Him?

Who do we look like?

Living Water

*If any man is thirsty, let him come to Me and drink.
He who believes in Me, as the Scripture said, "From
his innermost being shall flow rivers of living water.*
—John 7:37-38 NASB

Horticulturists tell us that plants thrive on
slow, deep watering that wets the earth to a depth of
four to six inches. Then when dry weather hits, the
plants are more likely to survive, even if they receive
water only once a week. Also, watering in the evening
hours decreases the evaporation factor that steals
moisture from the plants. One thing is certain, healthy
plants that produce lush foliage and beautiful fruit or
flowers demand plenty of water carefully applied to
their roots. Plant experts say the occasional sprinkling
here and there seems to do more damage than good.

Just as plants get thirsty, we get thirsty, too. When
the Samaritan woman at the well met Jesus, He
explained to her that physical water is temporary, but

spiritual water is eternal (John 4:13-14). To bear fruit, we need the living water of Christ dwelling within. If we're always in a hurry and just read a Bible verse here and there, our roots remain shallow and can wither in dry seasons. Through more extended times alone with God in prayer and in reading His Word, we develop inner sustenance for trials that come.

When we let God put His Living Water in our hearts, not only does He satisfy our spiritual thirst, He helps us to grow. And we can be a nourishing fountain to others.

Larkspur Lives

Sing to the Lord a new song; sing to the Lord, all the earth.
Sing to the Lord, praise his name; proclaim his salvation
day after day. Declare his glory among the nations,
his marvelous deeds among all peoples.
—Psalm 96:1-3

Pauline misread the instructions for planting larkspur seeds and placed the seeds too close together. When the larkspurs emerged from the soil, they looked like a tiny hedge of carrot tops. They seemed so whimsical; she didn't have the heart to thin them as much as perhaps she should have.

Despite her haphazard gardening procedures, Pauline found that the larkspur sprouted and grew in abundance. When a slight breeze ruffled through them, she was sure she heard tiny giggles of joy because the larkspurs knew God had created their beauty.

Their tall flower stalks formed a chorus of pink, blue, white, purple, and occasional splashes of lilac singers. The larkspur choir sang a new song of praises that delighted Pauline's soul. Flowers have the delightful capacity to sing songs for the eyes instead of the ears. The larkspurs stood tall and straight like vertical musical staffs filled with trills of colored notes all the way up their stalks.

As Pauline cut the mature ones for drying, even more larkspurs shot up and bloomed. The flowers were still singing praises in her garden past the first few light frosts of fall.

Our Christian walk can be a larkspur life. We can daily sing praises to our Lord. We can strive to make our lives of faith an observable witness of God's marvelous deeds.

Can others hear you singing?

Child's Play

Until we all reach unity in the faith and in the knowledge
of the Son of God and become mature, attaining
to the whole measure of the fullness of Christ.
—Ephesians 4:13

Professional golfer Tiger Woods was considered one of the top players of the 1990's, with the potential to rank among the greatest of all time. Watching him line up a 40-foot downhill breaking putt, some may recall seeing him on the "Tonight Show" when he was about three years of age.

He was already showing a talent for the game, so a small putting surface was set up for him. A ball was placed in front of Tiger, about eight feet from the cup. He lined up the shot, putted, and missed.

Another ball was placed in the same position. He again prepared to putt—then picked the ball up, placed it 6 inches from the cup, and promptly sank the shot. Johnny Carson and the audience laughed and cheered to see a small child do what many adults would like to do. Of course, if he did that today, he would be ejected from the tournament.

A resident of a small town was once asked by a tourist: "Have any famous people been born here?" He replied, "No, only babies."

We all start out as "only babies," but our Creator has placed within us the greatest power in the universe: the ability to grow, day by day, as we respond to increasing challenges.

How will you meet your challenges today? You could grow more selfish, more reclusive, more pessimistic, or more filled with hate. Or, with the help of God, you can grow to be more understanding, optimistic, giving, and loving. You have been given this day to grow. Will you do it your way or His?

Sonlight in My Garden

But grow in the grace and knowledge of
our Lord and Savior Jesus Christ.
—2 Peter 3:18

Martha badgered Johnny all year to plant her a
garden. Finally, he agreed. Together they tilled the soil,
preparing it with the best additives, including peat moss,
landscape mix, soil conditioners, and bark mulch.

Martha disliked the flowers in her local nursery, so
she begged Johnny to let her order some unique
varieties out of a mail order catalog. Gingerly, she
selected each one, often choosing the most expensive
plants. *It will be the prettiest yard in the neighborhood,*
she thought. *No one can match these beauties.*

The tender plants arrived in the mail, and Martha
began working immediately. She planted and watered;
she fertilized; she watched, and she waited. But
nothing happened. One by one, the leaves turned

yellow and began to wilt. By the end of spring, not one plant remained. They all shriveled and died.

Martha wrote a scathing letter to the mail order nursery demanding her money back.

Two weeks later, she received a reply.

"Madam, your letter indicated you planted your flowers in a beautiful shady area and fed them the best nutrients possible. Your flowers failed to grow for the following reason: You planted them in the wrong place. You ordered flowers that must face the sun. Although you took great care to prepare the soil, without exception, these particular plants will die without sunlight. Next time, please read the directions before ordering your flowers and planting your garden."

Our lives are like that. We may spend great amounts of care and dollars to make ourselves beautiful. But if we are not facing the Son, we will wilt and eventually die. No amount of expensive "additives" will take the place of adequate Sonlight in our souls.

Bloom Where You Are Transplanted

You will be like a well-watered garden,
like a spring whose waters never fail.
—Isaiah 58:11

A young couple moved to a new city, far from family and friends. The movers arrived; the couple unpacked their belongings, and the husband started his job the following week. Each day when he arrived home, his wife greeted him at the door with a new complaint.

"It's so hot here."

"The neighbors are unfriendly."

"The house is too small."

"The kids are driving me crazy."

And each afternoon, her husband would hold her gently and listen to her gripes. "I'm sorry," he would say. "What can I do to help?"

His wife would soften and dry her tears, only to begin the same scenario the next afternoon.

One evening her husband walked through the front door with a beautiful flowering plant. He found a choice spot in the backyard and planted it. "Honey," he said. "Every time you feel discontented, I want you to go and look at your garden. "Picture yourself as that little flowering plant. And watch your garden grow."

Every week he brought home a new tree, flowering shrub, or rose bush and planted them in the backyard. His wife cut some flowers from the growing plants and took them to a neighbor. Each morning she watered the garden and measured its progress. Friendships grew with other women in her block, and they asked her for gardening help. Soon, they were seeking spiritual advice as well.

By the end of the next year, the couples' yard looked like a *Better Homes & Gardens* magazine feature.

Our Heavenly Father knows that we must all learn to bloom where we are transplanted. With His wise, loving touch, we will not only flourish, but we can produce the ever-blooming fruit of love, kindness, and contentment.

Working the Soil

The Lord is nigh unto them that are of a broken heart.
—*Psalms 34:18 KJV*

Even though her husband had been gone for
months now, Nana still missed Bill immensely.
Whenever her loneliness became too great, she would
head for the garage and her gardening tools. She and
Bill had a garden for as long as the grandchildren
could remember, and she was determined that they
would still have a garden even after Bill was gone.
Besides, it gave her life purpose, and it seemed as if
Bill were right there with her as she turned the soil,
planted the seeds, watered the seedlings, and weeded
and encouraged the plants to grow.

As she worked, she remembered the times they
had worked side-by-side. She recalled how she liked
to see the muscles in Bill's forearms ripple as he pulled
weeds, of how dark the dirt was against the tanned

skin of the backs of his hands, and of how he would always wipe the sweat from his face with a big red bandanna. Without much effort, she could even see again how the sunlight bounced off his wide-brimmed straw hat and the way his eyes would sparkle with anticipation as he spoke of the harvest to come.

She seemed to feel him nearby as she worked in the garden, and she often quietly murmured, "Bill, I know we will have some good tomatoes this year."

It is hard to experience more contentment than when you see the rewards of your work. Life is much the same in that sense—whether one is tending a garden, raising a child, or growing a marriage—it takes work. Whether alone or with a loved one, we always have the company of a special Companion throughout life's journey. Just ask Nana.

Texas Limestone

And other fell on good ground, and did yield fruit.
—Mark 4:8 KJV

Anita was determined to have a garden. She spent the entire hot, humid afternoon hacking away at the small plot of ground in the back of their central Texas home. In the vernacular of farmers, it was "poor" soil—incapable of sustaining even the hardiest of vegetables. After about three inches, the soil gave way to limestone. But that was not going to stop her! She just grew more stubborn as she shoveled her way through the rocks.

Every time it seemed that she had found the last rock, sparks would fly from the blade as she again struck limestone. She grew weary and was tempted to give up her garden. The ground was just too hard and the soil too scarce. It seemed that nothing would grow in this place. Yet she longed for a garden filled with ripe red tomatoes, green cucumbers, tall okra, and big ears of corn.

Slowly, the soil began to turn more easily. Occasionally, she would use the garden hose to dampen the dry earth as she removed the rocks. Finally the rocks were removed. She then mixed in bags of new, rich topsoil and shaped the soil into nice smooth, parallel rows. At last, the garden was ready for her to plant the vegetable seeds.

Like her garden, Anita had to work hard to keep her heart right and free from the burdensome rocks of unforgiveness. She longed for healthy, merciful soil where seeds of God's love would yield a bumper crop of compassion and kindness. She knew that her daily choices in thought, word, and deed would determine whether her heart-garden was full of bitter rocks or joyful vegetation.

"Forgiveness is not an occasional act, it is a permanent attitude."—Martin Luther King, Jr.

How does your garden grow?

Small Yet Tall

But in all these things we overwhelmingly
conquer through Him who loved us.
—Romans 8:37 NASB

David was a shepherd boy who faced the fierce Philistine giant, Goliath. His enormous opponent was armed and seemed to be well-prepared to meet his enemy in battle. Goliath had seen many battles before. He was a warrior, but often he relied solely on his size and ferocity to win the battle before weapons were even drawn. He was the Philistines' icon of strength.

Mocking laughter could be heard all over the countryside when this powerful, tall, well-developed warrior stood there facing a boy. How could this be? Surely Goliath had the upper hand. He was the strongest and the best the Philistines had.

What did David bring to this battle? He was a boy, untrained in the weapons of warfare. He did not stand a chance. He was too young. For David's people, this seemed to be yet another disaster waiting to happen.

While Goliath mocked God, David worshipped the Lord. Goliath was smug in his sure victory; David asked God for a miracle. Goliath trusted his size and strength to save him; David relied on Someone far bigger and stronger. Though small, David trusted in a Mighty God. One tiny stone defeated the giant.

For thousands of years, tiny seeds planted in the cold, dark earth have yielded bumper crops of vegetation, towering trees, and every imaginable flowering plant. Faith plants a seed and looks for the harvest. David threw a stone and looked for a victory.

From a Tiny Seed

*And other seeds fell into the good soil and as
they grew up and increased, they yielded a crop
and produced thirty, sixty, and a hundredfold.*
—Mark 4:8 NASB

The story goes that a century ago a German
princess lay dying. While on her deathbed she
requested that her grave be covered with a large
granite slab and that stone blocks be placed all around
the slabs to seal the grave. She also gave orders for the
granite and stones to be held together with large
fasteners made of iron. At her request, the inscription
in the top of the stone read, "The burial place,
purchased to all eternity, must never be opened."

Apparently during the burial, a tiny acorn found
its way into the grave. Sometime later, a small shoot
began to push its way up through a thin crack in the
granite slab. The acorn was able to absorb in just
enough nourishment to grow. After years of growth,

the mighty oak tree broke through the aging iron clamps. The iron was no match for the oak, and the clamps burst, exposing the grave that was never to be opened. New life sprang forth from a deathbed and one tiny seedling.

Every day we are given numerous opportunities to take advantage of fresh new starts. New beginnings often come when something else has ended. When we allow sin to die in our hearts, we find new life in Christ. Perhaps it is no accident that the mighty oak, which is one of the tallest and strongest in the world, starts from a tiny little seed.

A Pathway Light

Thy word is a lamp to my feet, and a light to my path.
Psalm 119:105 NASB

Most gardens are lighted with small outdoor lanterns that glow just enough to keep visitors from stumbling along the path. At one garden I visited in St. Augustine, Florida, tiny white lights trimmed a centrally located gazebo. Large umbrella-like trees, draped with strings of lights like twinkling diamonds, extended the romantic atmosphere.

Even the smallest light in the right location can illumine a large area. Such is the case in Israel's museum to honor the children who were killed in the Holocaust. Only six candles light the museum. How? Because they are strategically placed in front of various-angled mirrors, magnifying the flames and casting light throughout the rooms.

A Pathway Light

In the 1800's, a monk named Walter Denham in Belgium placed a candle on top of each one of his well-worn leather shoes. Then with the candles lighted, he could overcome the darkness of the cold stone abbey one step at a time.

Perhaps you are in a set of dark circumstances now—either something you cannot control or habits that you cannot break. You may just feel lonely and empty inside. Just as Walter used the candles to light his way, you can find your spiritual way.

Do you need light for your soul today? Relying on God for assistance is like reaching for a lamp in the darkness. As morning light dispels the dark night, the Word of God exposes darkness in our hearts and illumines truth about a Heavenly Father who cares.

Darkness is the absence of light. But since God is light, then in Him there is no darkness at all.

Flower Power

*For we dare not make ourselves of the number, or compare
ourselves with some that commend themselves: but they
measuring themselves by themselves, and comparing
themselves among themselves, are not wise.*
—2 Corinthians 10:12 KJV

Butchart Gardens is one of the most famous
tourist attractions in Victoria, British Columbia. The
elaborate display dates back to 1904 when Jenny
Butchart decided to transform part of her husband's
limestone quarry into a sunken garden. Today it is
open all year and includes a botanical array of
breathtaking beauty.

When one walks through these delightful grounds,
it is impossible to choose the most outstanding
exhibition. The plants are obviously healthy and well
attended. Each provides colorful blossoms that are
distinct, yet make a significant contribution in the
overall scheme and design.

Likewise, part of our spiritual growth is to realize our importance in God's garden, especially when we exercise the talents and abilities He has given. Many feel inferior about their own gifts and they compare themselves unfavorably with others. And yet God designs different people just as He created various kinds of flowers. The lily and the rose each have their own features. In fact, every blossom has its own unique characteristics. Tulips and lilacs and hyacinths are not alike and yet each kind of flower adds a particular fragrance and beauty to any arrangement.

The same is true in life. Take a few moments to make an inventory of your gifts. Then ask the Holy Spirit to guide you. Through His power, you can make a difference in the lives of others as well as your own.

Dear Father, thank You for helping me to grow so that my blossoms will make the world's landscape more beautiful.

Wildflower Worth

*Look at the lilies and how they grow. They don't work or
make their clothing, yet Solomon in all his glory was not
dressed as beautifully as they are. And if God cares so
wonderfully for flowers that are here today and gone
tomorrow, won't he more surely care for you?*
—Luke 12:27-28 NLT

℘ach spring, wildflowers bloom in profusion at a
place in Idaho called "Craters of the Moon."
Nourished by snowmelt and occasional rains, the
flowers spring up in the lava rock left by an eons-old
volcano. It is a stunning sight to see the small, delicate
wildflower blossoms bursting into life amid the huge,
rugged boulders.

Sightseers can follow footpaths all through the
lava rocks to discover the surprising spots that dusty
maiden, dwarf monkey flower, and indian paintbrush
find to grow. The life span for the fragile flowers can
be as brief as one day if the hot desert winds blow into

the area. Even without the winds, three weeks is about their longest show.

When Jesus taught His followers, He often sat outside. Perhaps He sat on a Judean hillside among the spring wildflowers when He pointed at the lilies, encouraging the worriers not to be blinded to the fact that God takes care of all His creation, even a short-lived wildflower. If He takes care of them, He certainly will care for us.

How do we avoid worry? By increasing our faith in our God who loves us. By starting each day focusing on Him instead of our fears, and remembering His loving care even for the brief life of a wildflower.

The Contest

*And the child grew and became strong, filled
with wisdom; and the favor of God was upon him.*
—Luke 2:40 RSV

It was a typical day in first grade, and while
their teacher was tending to other students, Sammy
and Molly were engrossed in a discussion of the
utmost importance: Who was taller?

Molly was one of the smaller children in the class,
but that never interfered with her keen sense of
competition. When Sammy declared his superior
height, she responded by sitting up tall and straight.

When Sammy sat up taller and straighter, Molly
stood up beside her desk.

When Sammy stood up across the aisle and
immediately overshadowed her, Molly—after stealing a
glance across the room to ensure her teacher's back
was still turned—stepped up on her chair.

When the teacher finally turned to check on the commotion, the two children were standing atop their desks, on their tiptoes, stretching for all they were worth!

Children are typically excited about getting bigger, and the wise adult still seeks growth. Those who lose this zest die long before their funerals.

How long has it been since you felt the thrill of growing—of improving some aspect of your life? You may have felt it as you graduated from high school, received your first promotion on the job, learned a new craft, or ran in your first 5K race. The desire for growth is a powerful incentive in our lives.

If improving in size, career, or talent is exciting, other aspects of our lives can bring even more lasting satisfaction. Growing in our relationship with God is one of them. In fact, taking our desires for growth to the Lord can result in a double blessing—gaining His strength and vision for improving our lives, while deepening our joy in knowing Him.

A Garden of Hope

*See, I am doing a new thing! Now it
springs up; do you not perceive it?*
—Isaiah 43:19

As Shannon sat by her mother's bedside day by
day, she observed the leaves change to autumn
splendor outside the bedroom window. And each day,
she watched her mother's cancer-riddled body weaken.

One by one, the green leaves outside faded to
yellow, then bright orange, covering the ground like a
pool of liquid sunshine. One morning a north gust of
wind blew through the back garden where the oak
tree stood. Its limbs, now naked and lonely, swayed in
the winter breeze.

As Shannon looked out the window one morning,
she noticed a lone leaf hung on tenaciously. The same
day, her mother's pulse grew weaker and she slipped
into a coma. All that week, Shannon struggled. She

longed to hear her mother's words once again—to feel the springtime of her voice, and to whisper "I love you" again to her mother.

Outside the bedroom window, the lone leaf held on. Shannon wondered how it could keep from fluttering to the ground. An inner voice seemed to murmur the answer: "It needs to let go, and so do you."

The next morning Shannon walked quietly into her mother's room dreading to see her mother's lifeless form. But her mom suddenly woke up, squeezed her daughter's hand, and said, "I love you, Shannon."

"Oh, Mom. I love you too."

And then, like a leaf that had clung too long, her mother released Shannon's hand—and she was gone.

As Shannon closed the drapes that afternoon, she realized the leaf had disappeared from the old oak tree. But in its place, a new bud was already forming. Shannon knew joy would blossom again. Like the promise of springtime, God would grow a new garden of hope in the fertile soil of Shannon's heart.

Uproot the Tree

"There . . . is a time to plant and a time to uproot."
—*Ecclesiastes 3:1-2*

After months of searching, a lawyer and his wife bought a house. They loved everything about it, especially the shady backyard. The contract went well—until the inspector finished his examination of the foundation.

"You have a tree growing too close to the house," he said. "If you don't remove it, the roots will eventually erode the foundation and cause it to shift. First, you'll see cracks on the inside walls, and then a major break on the outside brick structure. If you uproot the tree now and start watering the foundation regularly, the problem will correct itself—a minor cost of $500 for tree removal.

The lawyer's wife grew angry. "The reason we wanted this house was because of the trees, especially *that* one! We'll take our chances!"

So they moved in. They planted an expensive garden underneath the tree and enjoyed the shade all year long. One day, the lawyer noticed large cracks on the inside walls, and a jagged line followed the two-inch split in the outside brick wall—only a few feet from the tree roots.

The disgusted lawyer listed the house for sale immediately, but no one would buy the home. Finally, two years later, a realtor found a buyer with one condition: the owners repair the house before the sale.

By this time, the foundation needed a complete restoration. The cost? Just over $10,000. Eager to move out, the lawyer paid the money and sold the house at a substantial loss.

Like the lawyer's shade tree, little problems in life often appear harmless. If we ignore God's warnings to pull them up by the roots, those problems will eventually grow large enough to erode our spiritual foundation. We can avoid needless costly mistakes by listening—and heeding—God's words.

❀ • *69* • ❀

I Forgive You

But grow in grace.
—*2 Peter 3:18 KJV*

The cause of Jim's anger had long since been forgotten, but he continued to rail at his young son Ricky. He couldn't seem to stop himself. He was just so frustrated with the boy. On and on he went until finally he had exhausted his anger, and then he immediately felt guilty for his behavior.

Looking deep into Ricky's tear-filled eyes, Jim said, "Son, I am so sorry that I lost my temper. I was wrong to scream at you, and I was wrong to become so angry regardless of your actions. Will you please forgive me?"

Without a moment's hesitation, Ricky responded, "It's all right Dad, Jesus forgives you, and so do I!"

And then Ricky immediately launched himself into his father's arms for a hug. They remained that way for a couple of moments as the healing balm of forgiveness washed over them both. They had a special bond that was strong enough to stand the tests of parenting and growing up, a bond that was made stronger still by their shared faith. It seemed that Ricky's growing up was also forcing Jim to deal with his own childish behaviors and to make some changes.

Jim was acutely aware that his every action was scrutinized by his young son, and he wanted to be a good father. He asked God to help him be a good example. He still struggled with his temper and impatience, but he committed himself to change his behavior. The words of his young son humbled and encouraged him.

"It's all right Dad, Jesus forgives you, and so do I!" He heard again.

Worthy or not, we are forgiven if we ask.

Life Lessons

But speaking the truth in love.
—*Ephesians 4:15* KJV

"You know that what you did was wrong, don't you?"

The words echoed in Sandra's mind as she went home from school that evening. She was a good student who had never cheated in her life. Yet, this last assignment had been more than she could do. In a moment of desperation, she copied the work of another student.

Her teacher, Mrs. Wallace, had asked her to wait after class, and Sandra knew what was coming. Still, it was a shock when Mrs. Wallace asked her if it was really her work.

"Yes," she squeaked out, then wondered why she had lied.

Looking her straight in the eye, Mrs. Wallace carefully said, "You know that what you did was wrong, don't you? Take tonight to think about your answer, and I will ask you again in the morning if this is your work."

It was a long night for Sandra. She was a junior in high school with a well-deserved reputation for honesty and kindness. She had never cheated before, and now she had compounded her mistake by deliberately lying—and to someone she admired and loved. The next morning she was at Mrs. Wallace's classroom door long before school officially started, and she quietly confessed her misdeed. She received the appropriate consequences, a zero on the assignment and detention (her first and only detention).

Years later, Sandra often thought of that experience and felt gratitude for loving correction from someone she respected. Mrs. Wallace was willing to help Sandra make honest choices—even on the heels of making a dishonest one. For Sandra, this was a life lesson about taking responsibility for past mistakes and choosing honesty no matter what the consequences.

Storytellers

*And thou shalt teach them diligently unto thy
children, and shalt talk of them where thou sittest
in thine house, and when thou walkest by the way,
and when thou liest down, and when thou risest up.*
—Deuteronomy 7:7 KJV

The Polynesians are strong believers in the
importance of teaching the next generation the history
of their families. They sit around and "talk story." They
speak with excitement and their eyes twinkle as they
tell the young ones about their ancestry. The younger
generation sits in rapt attention, soaking up every
detail. The history of these families is passed down in
story form that anyone can easily understand. The
children pay special attention so that when they grow
up, they will be able to pass the family history down
to another generation.

A 1998 blockbuster animated film, *The Prince of
Egypt,* tells once again about the Israelites' escape from

slavery and their search for a land of freedom and abundance. Modern Jews still tell stories as part of their Passover celebration. Traditionally, the youngest child asks why certain foods are eaten and certain traditions are practiced. The answers are told in story form, reflecting on events thousands of years ago and passed on generation to generation.

Jesus taught by telling stories that even the youngest, most uneducated, and least experienced could understand. Now, more than 2,000 years later, those parables are still told. Stories about a wayward son, about planting seeds, about searching for a lost coin, and about showing kindness to others are timeless messages about the Kingdom of God.

Aesop's Fables, fairy tales by the Brothers Grimm, and stories by Hans Christian Andersen are memorable not only for their messages but also for their interesting characters and events. If a picture is worth a thousand words, then a story must be worth a thousand pictures.

How Firm a Foundation

*The rain came down, the streams rose, and the winds
blew and beat against that house; yet it did not fall,
because it had its foundation on the rock.*
—Matthew 7:25 NIV

The world's tallest tower stands in Toronto,
Ontario, Canada. The first observation deck rises to
1,136 feet and the second is even higher at 1,815 feet.
Photographs and information located inside the tower
help visitors comprehend the enormous undertaking
of the project. Sixty-two tons of earth and shale were
removed from fifty feet into the ground for laying the
concrete that rises to the sky.

From 1972 to 1974, 3,000 workers were at the
tower site. Harnessed by safety ropes, some of the
laborers dangled outside the giant for their finishing
work. Remarkably, no one sustained injuries nor died
on location.

Today a rapid elevator transports visitors upward for a breathtaking view of the city and all surrounding areas. Many say, "It was worth the money, time, and effort required to build the CN Tower."

We, too, need a good foundation for facing life each day. As we pray and spend time with our Heavenly Father, we are strengthening our spiritual foundation, our support base for life. We are able to see more from His point of view and not just our own. Thus we are not overwhelmed by whatever comes our way. When we feel we're hanging on the edge or suspended in mid-air, we can take courage in knowing He is holding us—firmly planted—in the palm of His hand. His foundation is strong and sure, and He will not crumble and fall.

A Garden in the Mountains

And why are you anxious about clothing? Observe how
the lilies of the field grow; they do not toil nor do
they spin, yet I say to you that even Solomon in
all his glory did not clothe himself like one of these.
—Matthew 6:28-29 NASB

After the mountains of Alaska begin shedding
their heavy white coats, the tundra bursts forth in
bloom. No one plants flowers on the mountainside,
but wildflowers are as predictable as spring itself. Blue
lupine, bright pink fireweed, and many other colorful
varieties announce that winter has departed. Dark,
gloomy days are gradually replaced with more and
more light. By midsummer, the days extend almost
until dawn. In the twilight's glow, this mountain garden
flourishes along endless miles of pristine wilderness.

Every time the sun rises, the seasons change, and
the flowers bloom, all of nature seems to be
announcing, "God is faithful." In a world of man-made

chaos, God is dependable, not only in matters of creation, but in our personal lives as well. Remembering God's dependability is helpful, especially when circumstances are not going our way.

When divorce rips the marriage vows or the doctor diagnoses cancer or the telephone call delivers shocking news, we often wonder if God has forgotten us. Yet when we reflect upon the past events of our lives, we can trace His faithful provision. Just as He adorns the lilies of the field, He will take care of our concerns. So, we need not be anxious. When difficulties arise, we can pray, knowing the Master Gardener is always there, year in and year out.

Like spring follows winter and renews a harsh landscape, our Jehovah Jireh—the Lord who provides—brings peace to still the turmoil in our hearts and newfound joy with the blessing of each day.

Flowerbox Faith

On my bed I remember you; I think of you through the watches of the night. Because you are my help, I sing in the shadow of your wings. My soul clings to you; your right hand upholds me.
—Psalm 63:6-8

One Labor Day weekend, Shannon's husband constructed a large flowerbox for her. With great care, she picked out and purchased two hundred top-quality bulbs. Next, she filled the flowerbox with the perfect mixture of soil, fertilizer, and peat moss. Then, she spent hours planting the bulbs in a delightful design.

All through the long Idaho winter, she thought about her tulips, daffodils, and hyacinths. If they followed God's plan and waited for His perfect timing, they would change from dull, brown clumps into colorful celebrations of spring.

Maintaining our faith in God during times of forced inactivity is similar to a dormant bulb planted in a flowerbox. At certain times in our lives, we may be compelled to stop all activity and take time out to heal. Instead of lying in our beds fretting about our restraining circumstances, we simply need to wait and rest.

Dormancy for a bulb is nature's solution to getting through times of difficult weather conditions. God's gift of rest is His way of helping us through difficult health conditions. All bulbs store food to carry them through their dormant periods. We can use our times of dormancy to nourish our souls by planting our hearts in the fertile soil of His Scriptures.

Like bulbs waiting for spring, we can rest in God's promises as we wait for our recovery. We can look forward to the certain celebration of life through Christ. He alone will bring the colors of spring to our souls.

The Beauty of Discipline

Blessed is the man you discipline, O LORD,
the man you teach from your law.
—Psalm 94:12

The ancient Chinese art of *bonsai* (pronounced bone-sigh) has existed as a horticultural art form for nearly 2000 years. The word *bonsai* literally means, in both the Chinese and Japanese languages, *tree-in-a-pot*. Practiced all over the world, bonsai is a sublime art where shape, harmony, proportion, and scale are all carefully balanced, and the human hand works in a common cause with nature.

A tree planted in a pot is not a bonsai until it has been pruned, shaped, and trained into the desired shape. Bonsai are kept small by careful control of the plant's growing conditions. Only branches that are important to the bonsai's overall design are allowed to remain, while unwanted growth is pruned away. The bonsai roots are confined to a pot and are periodically clipped.

The shape of these trees is always as found in nature. Some bonsai have been known to live for hundreds of years, and the appearance of old age is much prized. The living bonsai will change through seasons and years, requiring pruning and training throughout its lifetime. And as time goes on, it will become more and more beautiful.

In truth, the bonsai would be nothing more than your average tree, but for the discipline of the artist. Giving constant attention to the direction of growth, trimming away what is ugly or unnecessary, and strengthening the most vital branches result in a work of art that brings beauty to its surroundings for many years.

In our own lives, it is that same discipline that makes the difference between your average life and one that brings joy and beauty to its surroundings. With God's Word as our discipline, we too can become works of art.

Secret Gardens

*This land that was laid waste has
become like the garden of Eden.*
—Ezekiel 36:35 NIV

The Secret Garden, by Frances Hodgson Burnett,
beautifully illustrates the power of kindness and faith.
Collin, the adolescent son of a rich, but grieving father
who cannot rebound from his wife's death, lives his
days as a demanding, selfish invalid. At first, Collin
rejects the friendly gestures of Mary, his long-lost
cousin. When young Mary discovers the key to a
secret garden on the grounds of her uncle's estate, she
also opens a hidden door to her own heart's joys. She
immediately sets out to restore the garden's long-lost
magic and beauty.

Little by little, Mary persuades Collin to take another
step toward healing and unselfishness. Her stubborn
persistence finally prevails on Collin to spend time
outside in the restored garden, which had been lovingly

planted by his late mother. Strength seeps back into the young boy's life and changes his saddened, bitter heart. The garden seems to work like magic on the young boy as he is restored, not only in body and spirit, but in relationship with his distant father.

Untended gardens can hide for years, as bitter thorns grow, choking out the life and obscuring their beauty. But as we gently clear away the rubble of the past and cut through the neglected gardens of their hearts, we make a remarkable discovery—lives, sweet and beautiful, waiting to be filled with the divine fragrance of heaven. There are potential "gardens" all around us—in our neighborhoods, in our schools, in our homes, and at work. We have been given the key, and it is no secret what virtual gardens of Eden we can help uncover as we share God's love freely with others.

Smell the Roses

*Listen for God's voice in everything you do, everywhere
you go; he's the one who will keep you on track.*
—Proverbs 3:6 THE MESSAGE

*I*n his book *Seasons of Life*, Charles Swindoll
tells the following story about the defender of the
theory of evolution, the famous biologist and devoted
disciple of Darwin, Thomas Henry Huxley:

> "Having finished another series of public assaults
> against several truths Christians held sacred, Huxley
> was in a hurry the following morning to catch his train
> to the next city. He took one of Dublin's famous horse-
> drawn taxis and settled back with his eyes closed to rest
> himself for a few minutes. He assumed the driver had
> been told the destination by the motel doorman, so all
> he had said as he got in was, 'Hurry…I'm almost late.
> Drive fast!' The horses lurched forward and galloped
> across Dublin at a vigorous pace. Before long Huxley
> glanced out the window and frowned as he realized

they were going west, away from the sun, not toward it.

"Leaning forward, the scholar shouted, 'Do you know where you are going?' Without looking back, the driver yelled a classic line, not meant to be humorous, 'No, your honor! But I am driving very fast!'

"As Rollo May, the contemporary psychologist, once admitted: 'It is an old and ironic habit of human beings to run faster when we have lost our way.'"[5]

Garden-tending requires time—a slowing down of our breakneck speeds. Taking time to "smell the roses"—especially lingering near the fragrance of the Rose of Sharon—helps us to receive God's clear directions on where we are really headed in life. If we will head toward the Son with a listening ear and give up speeding to meaningless destinations, we will discover a purposeful life, filled with good things from the Master Gardener.

Black Mountain

Many are the plans in a man's heart, but
it is the Lord's purpose that prevails.
—Proverbs 19:21

"I will just run away to Black Mountain!"
screamed five-year-old Richard.

"Okay, if that's what you want, go ahead,"
responded his mother, opening the door and ushering
him out to the front porch.

The silence descended on him like a cloak. The
sun was long gone, and full night had settled upon the
landscape. By the starlight he could just make out the
dark form of Black Mountain to the north. Somewhere
in the darkness, he heard the scurrying of a small
animal and then the flap of wings in the night sky.

Suddenly, his small heart was pounding in his
chest and his breath was coming quicker. Going to
Black Mountain seemed like a real bad idea.

He thought, *Why did I say that?*

He sat on the porch with his knees drawn up to his chest and arms clasped around them. A tear trickled down his cheek as he tried to fight off his fears.

From the kitchen, he heard his father ask, "Richard, would you like to come to supper with the rest of us now?"

Sometimes when we get angry with ourselves, at others, at circumstances, or even at God, we want to run away. We stomp out our anger, and we make threats. We go out on the porch and pout. Yet, the Father waits patiently and even calls to us to rejoin the family. Love chases away fears, and restoration heals hurts.

Ripe Cantaloupes

It is good that a man should both hope and quietly wait.
—*Lamentations 3:26* KJV

Rita and James could scarcely wait to pick the cantaloupes. The children had worked hard preparing the soil, planting, watering, pulling weeds, and keeping the bugs out of their garden. Now, with small cantaloupes on the vines, it had become pure torture to wait for the tender fruit to mature and grow.

Early on, they would venture out daily to see if things were growing yet. But every morning was an exercise in patience. All they could see was dirt—nothing but bare dirt!

Then one day, tiny green shoots had shoved aside the earth and were emerging from the soil. Fuzzy cantaloupe vines began to spread across the small hills at the rear of the garden—soon to bear melons.

"Dad, this one's ready to pick, I just know it is!" James cried.

"Nope, I am afraid not," Dad replied. "It may look big enough to pick, but it is not ripe yet. Don't you see how green it still is?"

Once Dad left, they could not wait anymore. They picked the melon. Alas, just as Dad had warned, the hard melon was far from ripe. When they told him later, he quietly laughed.

The next week, he came to them, and said, "Hey, would you two like some fresh, homegrown cantaloupe?" Their faces lit up with excitement, and the trio ventured to the garden where Dad pointed out two beautifully ripened melons for them to pick.

Rita grinned at her father between bites of melon and said, "It sure tastes better when we wait for the right time to pick the cantaloupe, doesn't it, Dad?"

Being patient for God's perfect timing can be difficult. But it's always worth the wait.

Time for Bed

Teach me thy way, O Lord.
—*Psalm 27:11* KJV

When children are around two years old, many of them decide that staying up past their regular bedtime is something worth creating havoc over. These little replicas of ourselves come up with every conceivable excuse to stay awake, no matter how tired they may actually be. From the tenth drink of water, to the fifth bathroom trip, to the whining about what's behind the door (or under the bed), to the "I love you sooooo much, Mommy and Daddy", to the fits of anger—these little ones try to get something that they can't yet handle responsibly.

Parents read books, complain to their child's pediatrician, consult with their minister, whine to their own friends, and disagree with their spouse about the right way to handle this annoying situation. In some cases the child may gain the upper hand and stay up too late, smiling gleefully while sitting between Mom and Daddy on the sofa watching TV and eating popcorn.

At this stage in their lives, two-year-olds are test-driving their ability to assert their own opinions and desires, the first step to autonomy. It is the parents' responsibility to guide those desires with a balance of freedom and discipline. Physiologically, two-year-olds need more sleep than ten-year-olds or thirty-year-olds. Their growing bodies need time to rest in order to properly support each day's whirlwind of activity. The privilege of staying up later truly is only something that can be earned with time.

Like toddlers, sometimes we want something that we are not yet prepared to handle. We might not like it much, but sometimes we just have to trust God to know what is best for us. If we ask God for wisdom in balancing our lives, He is sure to help us.

Let Me Do It by Myself!

Train up a child in the way he should go,
even when he is old he will not depart from it.
—Proverbs 22:6 NASB

Five-year-old Lili would often fluctuate from "Let me do it by myself" to "Mommy, help me," in a matter of moments. Tying her shoes, buttoning her sweater, pouring her milk, riding her bicycle, and brushing her hair seemed to be her rites of passage.

Her mother seldom knew whether it was all right to lend unsolicited assistance or to let the youngster work independently. When safety was an issue, the answer was obvious. "No, Honey. Mommy has to help you with baking cookies (or crossing the street or reaching a top shelf), because I don't want you to get hurt. When you're bigger, you can do this by yourself." Because Lili was allowed lots of opportunities to do the safe things on her own, it helped to take the sting out of the temporary *no* she got on the unsafe ones.

We say *no* to our children because we love them. And when the time is right, we can also say *yes* because we love them. It takes wisdom and knowledge to train a child. *No* might be the best answer to a request today that might change to a *yes* tomorrow after some instruction and practice.

Growing up is not easy. We have life lessons from cradle to grave. Like our children, we need guidance in knowing how to do certain things. While we always need God's help, some decisions or circumstances require double doses of His guidance.

From that first "no-no" spoken to a toddler who is about to touch a hot stove to that moment when we reluctantly slip the car keys into our teen's hand, are tucked away years of training. If we have taught and loved our children well, we can confidently say, "Yes, you and God can do it by yourselves."

Comfort in the Valley

*Even though I walk through the valley of the shadow
of death, I will fear no evil; for Thou art with me;
Thy rod and Thy staff, they comfort me.*
—Psalm 23:4 NASB

Several years ago, after the untimely death of her youngest son, Fran had to learn about trusting God. Sometimes she felt forsaken, lonely, and at times even angry that God allowed her seventeen-month-old to succumb to bacterial meningitis. Everything medically possible was done to no avail.

With time, God comforted her with the knowledge that her son is with Him and will be reunited with her someday. The Lord had called Fran to encourage others, even in the midst of her own pain and doubt, and help them understand that while our loved ones will always be in our hearts, our focus remains on the Lord Jesus Christ.

Fran had often read Psalm 23, but she never actually understood it until she visited Israel and saw the rugged terrain traversed by David and the shepherds. Many of the crevices on the rocky hills are so narrow and deep that the sun never shines all the way to the bottom. It remains a shadow. Certain death would result if anyone should fall in, because rescue would be virtually impossible. David's staff helped him walk with sure footing and the rod defended him from wild animals. Most of all, he became acutely aware of God's provision.

Through the valley times in our lives, we, too, can be sure that we are not alone. His presence is real. Jesus will still be there through all the pain and the changes in our life situations. Nothing is more comforting.

Stress and Serenity

And after He had sent the multitudes away,
He went up to the mountain by Himself to pray;
and when it was evening, He was there alone.
—Matthew 14:23 NASB

"*H*on," the petite supermarket employee said in her southern drawl, "everybody I know says they are *just worn out.*" She took a deep breath, brushed a wisp of unruly brunette hair away from her blue eyes, and continued checking groceries.

Stress has become a buzzword for Americans, especially in the last decade. At some point in our lives, we are all overcome with hectic schedules and perfectionistic tendencies.

In his article, "Confessions of a Workaholic," psychiatrist Paul Meier wrote,

> "Having grown up with an overdose of the Protestant work ethic, I was an honor student who was somewhat

*overzealous . . . I was a first-class workaholic and I
was proud of myself for being one. I thought that was
what God wanted of me."*[6]

But later through the help of friends, the
conviction of the Holy Spirit, and biblical teaching,
Dr. Meier established new priorities. At the top of his
list was: "Know God personally."

He observed, "I've learned to accept living in an
imperfect world. Every need is not a call for my
involvement. I have learned to trust God instead of
myself to rescue the world. He can do a much better
job of it anyway."

Jesus, too, must have been exhausted by demands
placed upon Him. When He departed to pray in quiet
solitude, He left a significant example for us to
follow—daily.

*Dear Father, help me to make quietness a priority so
that, regardless of the time of day, I can come to the
garden alone and hear Your voice.*

Bumper Crop

Do not be interested only in your own life,
but be interested in the lives of others. In your
lives you must think and act like Christ Jesus.
—Philippians 2:4-5 NCV

$\mathcal{D}$orothy wasn't allowed to plant a garden outside the townhouse they rented, so she decided to do the next best thing. She bought large pots and created a container garden on her patio.

One evening while she relaxed on their patio, her husband said, "Look! Our neighbor has tomatoes already. Why don't we?"

Much to her amazement, her neighbor had an abundance of fat green tomatoes covering her vines. All that Dorothy had growing were the tiny yellow flowers that promised fruit.

Dorothy had babied her plant by gently positioning it up the rungs of its tomato cage as it grew. She judiciously showered it with water, and moved the pots around for the best sunshine. Yet, all she had was a profusion of vines.

Dorothy searched through her gardening books and discovered that she needed to pinch back staked tomato plants. Pinching helps the plant focus its energy on producing its fruit instead of merely growing taller.

Many of us are like Dorothy's tomato plant. We love showing the abundant leaves of our spiritual insights. We take pride in how we are climbing the rungs of increased Bible knowledge. But do we only *promise* fruit? Do we apply what we've learned to our actions? Do we focus our energy on producing quality fruit?

When we pinch back our self-centeredness and concentrate on Christ, we might even grow a bumper crop of fruit to God's glory.

The Good Soil

It had been planted in good soil by abundant water so that it would produce branches, bear fruit and become a splendid vine.
—Ezekiel 17:8

An employee approached his employer and said, "I've had ten years of experience on this job, and I'm still making the same salary that I made when I started. It's time that I got a raise."

His boss retorted, "You haven't had ten years of experience. You've had one experience for ten years!"

Many of us feel that our lives could be described in the same way: one experience over and over again—or at best, boringly few experiences. When this is the pattern of our lives, we not only become depressed, but we also have no growth. Just as a garden needs fertilizer and nutrients to enrich its soil, we need the enrichment of activities and experiences to broaden our lives and stimulate our souls.

The Good Soil

Joseph Campbell once said, "I don't believe people are looking for the meaning of life as much as they are looking for the experience of being alive."

How, then, may we enrich our lives? It must be intentional. Don't think that someone else can do it for you. There are multitudes of ways to get started:

- Take up a sport that you always wanted to play.

- Take your spouse or a friend out to dinner and the entertainment of your choice.

- Plan a trip to see something or someone interesting.

- Volunteer to do work that will help the less fortunate.

- Visit a friend that you haven't seen for a while.

- Get involved in a place of worship that challenges you.

Participate! Learn! Sing! Read! Praise! Listen! Give! Talk with your God! In experiences such as these you will find the Source of all the excitement that you can handle.

When Faith Flutters

You who are spiritual should restore him gently.
—*Galatians 6:1*

Early one morning, Jill sat at her desk sorting through the previous day's bills.

Warm rays of spring sunshine streamed through her bedroom window, where she could view the backyard garden.

Out of the corner of one eye, Jill noticed a small, brownish butterfly go by—or so she thought. A few seconds later she turned to look at the window and saw that same butterfly had not landed on a plant; yet it seemed strangely suspended in midair. Its' wings fluttered helplessly, but the flying insect could not move.

Puzzled, Jill walked outside to get a closer look. Glistening in the sun, like a ladder of dew-dropped pearls, hung an almost invisible net. During the night, another one of nature's creatures—and one of the butterfly's enemies—had spun a magical web to trap its' victims.

Jill observed the struggle briefly until she watched the butterfly's wings grow motionless. She reached over and very gently plucked the winged insect from the spider's deadly threads. At first, the butterfly seemed stunned and fell to the ground. Jill gingerly picked it up and lifted it toward the sky, releasing its wings again. This time, it soared into the air and over the fence.

Anyone can tumble into tangled webs of deception. We believe a lie, follow the wrong leader, or confuse our priorities. Disillusionment sets in. Tired of the struggle, with faith fluttering, we can easily lose the strength to fight. At that point, a gentle, steady hand may be all we or someone else need to help free our fragile wings and send us soaring again on our heavenly way.

Flowers of Blessings

*How can we thank God enough for you in return for all
the joy we have in the presence of our God because of you?*
—1 Thessalonians 3:9

ℬill and Casey's grades were so close, that the
faculty asked them both to speak on graduation night
at Valley High School. Bill prided himself in being self-
made. For twenty minutes he enumerated his successes
and honors throughout high school. He ended by
emphasizing how much he deserved this honor.

A quiet, soft-spoken student, Casey thanked each
teacher who had contributed to her high school
education. Then she named friends and family
members who had influenced her and encouraged her
through many discouraging times. "These people are
the real stars," she said. "They believed in me when I
had no faith. They wished me success when I could

not dream. But most of all, I thank my God who has given me grace to come this far."

She continued, "With friends, loved ones, and God's help, you, too, can live your dream. Next year I will enter college and prepare to teach. Although I often wanted to quit, these heroes never did. I can never repay them for their generosity and kindness."

As a close friend gently pushed Casey in her wheelchair down the ramp, the entire student body gave Casey a standing ovation.

Oswald Chambers says, "Whenever you get a blessing from God, give it back to Him as a love-gift . . . if you hoard it for yourself, it will turn into spiritual dry rot . . . a blessing . . . must be given back to Him so that He can make it a blessing to others."

Like a grateful gardener, Casey had taken her "flowers" of blessings and presented them back to the ones who helped her grow them.

The Lost Cucumber

The harvest is past, the summer has ended.
—*Jeremiah 8:20*

"Wow, Dad can you believe the size of this cucumber," Danny nearly screamed as they walked through the family garden. They had been gone on vacation for over three weeks and the garden was somewhat overgrown. Since no one had been tending to it, many of the vegetables that should have been picked remained on the vine. One such vegetable was this large cucumber. It was the largest cucumber Danny had ever seen; but when he looked closer, he found that it was more golden than green, and it had rotten spots on the bottom where it lay touching the earth.

"Dad, we can't use this, it's not fit to eat. We needed to be here at least a week ago!"

Danny's father smiled at his son's exaggerated reaction and then remarked, "Yep, you're right. It is neat to see a cucumber this big, but we cannot use it for anything. We weren't here to watch for this cucumber, and now it's too late to pick it and to enjoy it."

Like the lost cucumber, life is often filled with "missed opportunities." The harvest of souls for the Kingdom of God requires we be watching and ready. Seeds sometimes bear fruit when we least expect it. We may fail to see opportunities because our attention is on things other than Him. Those opportunities become "could have," "should have," or "would have" regrets in our lives.

Four things come not back—the spoken word, the sped arrow, the past life, and the neglected opportunity.

—*Arabic Proverb*

Empty

I went past the ... vineyard of the man who lacks judgment;
thorns had come up everywhere, the ground was covered
with weeds, and the stone wall was in ruins.
—Proverbs 24:30-31

He was an angry man, cynical and mistrusting of others. He had been married seven different times in his life. He had a fair-sized nest egg put aside, and he was only a few years from retirement. But he did not seem to look forward to it.

His name was Charlie, and those who had known him early in his life said that he had not always been so difficult to get along with. They said that when he was young he was just irresponsible. But as he grew older and his life became characterized by failed relationships, he became bitter and angry.

Charlie's neighbors watched as his orchard suffered from neglect. The fence, fallen down in many places, was overgrown with wild vines. The untended orange trees grew ragged and without uniform shape, and down the rows between the trees, the weeds were knee-high, in some places, waist high. Rotting oranges were in evidence deep in the weeds. It had been a long time since anyone had paid attention to this orchard.

Charlie's life was like his orchard. In his book, *Man, the Dwelling Place of God*, A. W. Tozar wrote, "The untended garden will soon be overrun with weeds; the heart that fails to cultivate truth and root out error will shortly be a theological wilderness."[7]

Do you know a Charlie, whose spiritual garden only yields a bitter harvest? Ask the Master Gardener to use you to plant seeds of love and to send other laborers to help your "Charlie" enter a new season of hope and joy.

Forever Faithful

*And the LORD shall guide thee continually . . .
and thou shalt be like a watered garden, and like
a spring of water, whose waters fail not.*
—Isaiah 58:11 KJV

Jim Cymbala was a former college basketball player working in the business world of downtown Manhattan when his life took a dramatic turn. He had majored in sociology in college and had never been to Bible college, much less a seminary school, when he took the pastorate of a small church in New Jersey, at the urging of his father-in-law.

He did not consider himself a gifted or talented minister and preacher, but he was faithful to his father-in-law. And, when his father-in-law asked him to also serve as pastor for a second church, he again agreed. Eventually he and his wife determined that they could not pastor two churches, so they decided to stay with the second church—the smaller and less secure one. Over time he became discouraged at the lack of success.

Of that time he wrote, "I despaired at the thought that my life might slip by without seeing God show Himself mightily on our behalf."[8]

Prayer and persistence paid off. Jim Cymbala still serves as the pastor of that same church, the one that had less than thirty members when he took the pastorate more than twenty-five years ago.

Today, the church has more than 6,000 members and has started no less than twenty other churches.

It also has a pretty good choir led by Mrs. Jim Cymbala—the Grammy Award-winning Brooklyn Tabernacle Choir. The church and the choir provide astonishing evidence of the faithfulness of God. Faithfulness that benefits you just as it does Jim.

Landscapes

Therefore, my beloved brethren, be steadfast,
immovable, always abounding in the work of the Lord,
knowing that your toil is not in vain in the Lord.
—1 Corinthians 15:58 NASB

The landscapes around a home are usually very personal and reflect the individual taste of the home-owners. Making the outside reflect the owner is a unique talent landscape architects and novice gardeners have in common. Their work is so admired that friends and neighbors drive by, take pictures, and try to copy what these talented landscape artists create.

Landscaping is indeed an art, but it is much more. These eye-catching scenes say something about the owner. They express the preferences of the owner, giving insight into what is appreciated and worth all that effort to create.

Any gardener will tell you that even though they love gardening, it's still work. It involves investing money, hours of planning, and the hard work of creating the desired results. For the first year or two, a well-landscaped yard requires just about as much work as a new baby. If we are willing to follow the directions, invest in necessary materials, feed and water the garden plants, and battle the weeds, we can expect a lovely garden. It takes preparation and commitment—and a lot of hard work.

The way we live our lives expresses who we are and what we appreciate. It takes preparation, the nourishment of the Word, and constant attention to the weeds in our daily lives in order to create a beautiful and satisfying spiritual landscape.

Finding the Right "Home"

Those who wait for the Lord will gain new strength.
—Isaiah 40:31 NASB

A botanist, exiled from his homeland due to political unrest, took a job as a gardener in his new host country in order to support his family. His employer received a unique and rare plant from a friend. There were no care instructions with the plant so the man put it in one of his hothouses, thinking it would do well there.

Only a few days passed when he noticed the plant was dying. He called in his new gardener, the botanist, and asked if he had any ideas that might help to save the plant. The botanist immediately recognized this plant as an arctic variety that needed cold weather in order to survive. He took the plant outside in the frigid winter air and prepared the soil around it so the plant would gradually adjust to its new home. Almost immediately the plant went from wilting to vibrant.

Unaccustomed to the climate in the hothouse, the little plant must have felt the moisture draining from its small veins. The struggle to hold itself up to look the part of an expensive plant gave way under the weary load. The plant began to wilt and became only a shadow of its original beauty.

When the botanist rescued the plant and placed it in an environment suitable to its unique needs, the bowed-down foliage soaked in the nourishment and experienced renewal. Just like that rare plant, we can lose our spiritual strength if we live in an unhealthy environment. Seek God's help to find the right atmosphere for a joyous and productive life.

Tested by Fire

And He has said to me, "My grace is sufficient
for you, for power is perfected in weakness.
—2 Corinthians 12:9 NASB

Many gardens are outlined by evergreen
trees—some large and some small. The lodgepole pine
is a tall, stately tree found in the high Western
mountains. Commonly seen in Yellowstone National
Park, the hardwood is also valuable for making
railroad ties and poles. Its fragrant needle-shaped
leaves grow in bundles and produce fruit—a woody
pine cone, which takes two years to mature.

An interesting feature of the lodgepole is its
response to fire. When flames attack the tree, the heat
causes the cones to burst. The seeds are then
dispersed and natural reforestation occurs. New
growth begins and a fresh forest eventually replaces
the charred remains.

During life's trials, the fruit of our lives is also tested. Our spiritual maturity is revealed by how we respond. Do we see God's hand at work, even when our hearts are scorched by pain and sorrow? Have we become intimately acquainted with our Savior so that we know He will somehow use it for good?

When a young child was near death, friends gathered at the hospital to pray with the parents. Another mother, grieving over the loss of her own son, watched the praying group. She later received Christ as a result of the family's testimony. Both mothers shared a tremendous loss; but they also share a bright hope of one day seeing their boys again in Heaven.

After enduring the fires of adversity, we often learn that others have been watching with powerful results. Through trusting Him, their barren souls will burst into life and yield fruit for His glory.

One Lonely Seedling

*Let us not give up meeting together, as some are in
the habit of doing, but let us encourage one another.*
—Hebrews 10:25

One fall, Margaret decided to dig out a flowerbed
by her front door. After the first killing frost, she
yanked out the alyssum, tugged out the zinnias, and
hauled the cosmos to the compost heap. Then she
added fertilizer and mixed it into the dirt with her
rototiller.

The following April, as Margaret cleared out the
debris winter winds had blown into the flowerbed, she
discovered a solitary cosmos seedling struggling to
grow in a corner. The leggy and weak-stemmed
cosmos leaned toward the sun in a pathetic call for
help. Margaret couldn't imagine how the cosmos seed
managed to germinate after all her fall digging.

One Lonely Seedling

Margaret transplanted the single seedling into another bed with other baby cosmos. The flower grew strong and radiant within the cosmos congregation.

Like the one lonely seedling, we can't reach our full potential alone. Without being joined to a body of believers, spiritual growth can be one-sided or erratic. The transplanted cosmos worked with the other flowers to attract bees and butterflies. This made it possible for each flower to benefit. In the same way, believers are responsible for helping and encouraging each other for the benefit of all.

Joining with others strengthens our faith, expands our experiences, and refreshes our souls. This keeps us spiritually healthy. When we feel isolated or when we pull away from others, perhaps our lonely seedling needs a gentle transplanting.

The Rose and the Thorn

And Samuel grew, and the Lord was
with him and let none of his words fall.
—I Samuel 3:19 RSV

*T*here was a very cautious man

> *Who never laughed or played;*
> *He never risked, he never tried,*
> *He never sang or prayed.*
> *And when he one day passed away*
> *His insurance was denied;*
> *For since he never really lived,*
> *They claimed he never died![9]*

Progressing through life is so risky, and we all must face it at one time or another. In order to learn to walk, a toddler must risk painful falls time and again. The teen with his first driver's license immediately faces the most dangerous time of his driving career. The couple taking the vows of marriage must face the possibility that the very union they expect to bring life's greatest joy could also bring them their greatest heartache. And the entrepreneur trying to launch or expand her business knows that it could easily bring about a substantial loss.

Therefore, if there is such potential for pain in our attempts to grow and achieve throughout our lives, why do we even try?

One reason is that God has blessed us with an inner drive that compels us to improve our life. To paraphrase Anais Nin, *the day comes when the risk to remain tight in a bud is more painful than the risk it takes to blossom.* And we know that we cannot gather our beautiful roses without the possibility of being pricked by the thorns.

But when the prospect of facing those thorns seems too sharp and painful, remember that as God urges you to reach for new roses, you can also rely on His strength and guidance to help you manage your way through the thorns.

Miracle of Love

*This happened so that the work of
God might be displayed in his life.*
—John 9:3

A phone call one day changed May and Joe Lemke's life. Someone requested her help with a foster child. Her devotion as a nurse, combined with this English woman's gentle and tender love for children, had earned her the reputation of miracle worker, one which she would need for the challenge facing her that day.

The six-month-old infant boy named Leslie had been born severely retarded and with cerebral palsy. His doctors had removed both of his badly damaged eyes. May worked tirelessly and faithfully week after week, month after month, with virtually no change in the vegetable-like body.

She and her husband, now well into their sixties, continued their rituals of exercise, feeding, talking, and even playing music recordings for Leslie. When Leslie was thirteen they bought a piano, and May began to play simple songs for Leslie to hear. Still, no communication, no expression, nothing. But as May began to pray for God to give Leslie a talent, the parents noticed an intensity with which Leslie listened to music.

Then one day at age sixteen, Leslie dragged himself to the piano in his room, never having walked before, never having played a single note before, and played Tchaikovsky's "Piano Concert No. 1" flawlessly.

The Lemkes discovered Leslie could play anything after hearing it just one time. The miracles continued and one day the Lemkes heard his rich, baritone voice singing "How Great Thou Art." He learned to talk, to walk alone, to eat by himself.[10]

With God, nothing is impossible.

Butterfly Wings

*[Love] always protects, always trusts, always
hopes, always perseveres. Love never fails.*
—1 Corinthians 13:7-8

*H*ow do you find your place in the sun when
planted in the middle of fame? In *Seasons of Life*, Charles
Swindoll writes this of Anne and Charles Lindberg:

> "Anne was shy and delicate. Butterfly like. When she
> became Mrs. Charles Lindberg, Anne could have
> easily been eclipsed by her husband's shadow. She
> wasn't, however. The love that bound the two together
> for the next forty-seven years was tough love, mature
> love, tested by triumph and tragedy alike."

Anne describes how Charles Lindberg's love freed
her to become a woman of beauty:

> "To be deeply in love is, of course, a great liberating
> force and the most common experience that frees . . .
> Ideally, both members of a couple in love free each

*other to new and different worlds. I was no
exception to the general rule. The sheer fact of
finding myself loved was unbelievable and changed
my world, my feelings about life and myself. I was
given confidence, strength, and almost a new
character. The man I was to marry believed in me
and what I could do, and consequently I found I
could do more than I realized."*[11]

The security of her husband's love released Anne
to discover her own talents and gifts and to "emerge
from that cocoon of shyness a beautiful, ever delicate
butterfly" who would touch many lives.

Some marriages create cocoons of fear and
timidity in their spouses. They may squeeze their
partners from silk-like safety zones prematurely. Some
hover in the garden with a net, or treat their mates
like a specimen under glass—afraid their beloved
butterfly will discover wings and fly away.

But love, gentle and patient, knows that fragile
butterflies belong to the Lord. And when they are
given true wings, they never fly far from home.

"I Got It, I Got It"

*No discipline seems pleasant at the time . . . however,
it produces a harvest of righteousness and
peace for those who have been trained by it.*
—Hebrews 12:11

"No! No! No! That's not the way," hollered the coach as he watched what seemed like his entire T-ball team chase after the ball and then fight one another for it. While all of the outfielders and half of the infielders joyously wrestled for the baseball, the batter ran from base to base and finally crossed home plate.

The next batter stepped to the plate and promptly lofted the ball toward right center field. Immediately, all four outfielders screamed, "I got it," and the chase for the ball was on again. An instant replay, it seemed.

Again the coach yelled, "Same team, guys, we're all on the same team. Don't fight for the ball."

Although it did seem like chaos most of the time, the young boys and girls were learning the basics of the game of baseball and teamwork. By the year's end, progress had been made. The fights for the ball with teammates were far fewer and the players were learning to go to positions to await throws. In fact, at times they even recorded outs.

How did this happen? It happened as the coaches applied discipline and enforced rules during practice. At times, the players would get their feelings hurt and even cry when they were not allowed to participate because of misbehavior or unruliness. Yet, they did become better players.

The Christian walk also requires chastening if we are to progress from being unruly children to successful servants. Hannah Whitall Smith says it beautifully: "Look upon your chastening as God's chariots sent to carry your soul into the high places of spiritual achievement."[12]

What Am I Known For?

*For every tree is known by his own fruit. For of thorns men
do not gather figs, nor of a bramble bush gather they grapes.*
—Luke 6:44 KJV

"What does it matter what other people think of
me? I don't care about them anyway!" Rebecca blurted
out to her mom. "Why are you so concerned that I
finish the service project in Girl Scouts, anyway? I'm
gonna quit Scouts next year anyway, and besides I
already have plenty of badges."

"Scouting and badges are not the issues," her
mother replied. "I'm concerned with you and what
you are known for. You are very caring and
compassionate, warm and loving. You care deeply for
the welfare of others. You made a commitment to the
people at the assisted living facility and many of them
look forward to you visiting them. It's just hard for me
to see you not keeping a promise."

"But, I am tired of going up there every Saturday," Rebecca said.

Her mother suggested that they try to find a way to reduce some of her time commitment without abandoning the promise. Before long, Rebecca felt hopeful again that she could complete the commitment without giving up all of her free time.

Later she commented to a friend that she hoped she would always live up to her mom's belief in her to be caring, compassionate, and trustworthy.

We are known more by what we do than by what we say. Sometimes commitments are overwhelming, particularly during the holidays or when pressures at work or home or church or community seem to stretch us to the limit. Setting priorities and living by them—and most importantly, asking God for wisdom—will help us keep our promises without losing our heart.

Palm Salad

The righteous man will flourish like the palm tree.
—Psalm 92:12 NASB

The honeymooning couple crossed the long bridge from mainland Florida to Cedar Keys, a small island near central Florida. What an exciting ride along dirt roads lined with huge trees permanently bent in the same direction from the last major hurricane that hit the island with gale force winds. Friends had recommended they try the freshest and best seafood in Florida along with a bowl of the house specialty, palm salad. The drive was all the more pleasant because of the sweet anticipation of a good meal.

The presentation was exquisite; the food was delicious. The curious couple asked the waiter what part of the palm was used and how it was harvested. The islander explained that the scrub palm had to be cut so the leaves, thorns, and any parasites were removed. Using a machete to top the palm out to expose the deep part of its core, the harvester cuts deep inside the pulp to remove the heart of the palm, which is used for the salad. Such a deliberate and difficult act is performed many times a day so guests can enjoy the succulent palm salad.

Before the heart of the palm was discovered, no one could enjoy its tasty delight. No one knew it existed. What a shame to miss out on something so enjoyable!

May the eyes of our hearts be opened so that we can see—and savor—the blessings around us.

First Fruits

*Also you shall observe the Feast of the Harvest of the
first fruits of your labors from what you sow in the field.*
—Exodus 23:16 NASB

Gardening opens doors for learning and
produces a platform for teaching those around us
about God's great provision. Appreciating the elements
enough to tackle a garden opens our eyes to God's
creativity. Planning helps us to seek and accept God's
will for our lives. Tilling the soil and laboring to plant
and care for the garden teaches us responsibility and
good stewardship. Weeding is a reminder of the
spiritual battle we face each day. Waiting for the
harvest brings about patience.

Last but not least, reaping the harvest encourages
us to be thankful, and sharing the harvest brings
blessing to others and honors God.

Throughout history, God's people have been
taught to give the first fruits of their harvest as a

thanksgiving offering to God. In some cultures, a bountiful harvest is cause for great celebration. In the United States, the Thanksgiving tradition is based on sharing the harvest with others and giving thanks for God's rich blessings.

Sometimes the best way to give our first fruits to God means giving to those who are in need from our own abundance. Whether food or money, time or love, we can give what has been given to us. If done cheerfully and generously—with no strings attached— giving the first fruits of our labors brings rich reward.

God showers His blessing upon us, and the cycle of giving thanks and sharing the bounty begins again.

In everything the Lord gives, we can learn principles for our walk with Him if we will allow the lessons to become a part of the gift to us.

A Garden Fair

And their life shall be like a watered garden,
and they shall never languish again.
—*Jeremiah 31:12* NASB

When Pat's daughter needed financial support to do mission work in Hong Kong, she had an idea. Why not host a "Country Garden Fair," charge admission, and give the proceeds to the mission trip? Four hundred guests showed up to enjoy the breathtaking beauty of poppies, larkspur, delphiniums, hollyhocks, and other flowers in her four-acre English country garden. A year later at a second fair, the number of guests tripled. Pat honored her initial commitment and gave the proceeds to missions.

Later Pat took advantage of the high interest in her garden to hold an evangelistic outreach event. She desired that unbelievers would meet God and that existing believers would have a closer walk with Him. Guests admired the brightly colored flowers while listening to hymns and classical music, reading Scripture verses posted along the trails, and soaking up the peace and serenity of God's creation. The Garden Fair, which began as a way to meet a need, flourished as a creative way of planting spiritual seeds in numerous lives.[13]

Because life began in the first garden with Adam and Eve working the soil, we almost feel a pull to return to our roots. In a mysterious way, we feel at home when we dig and plant. Because of Pat's love for gardens, for God and for people, many can also look forward to someday strolling the grounds of their Heavenly Home.

God's Plan

*Then the L*ORD *God took the man and put him
into the Garden of Eden to cultivate it and keep it.*
—Genesis 2:15 NASB

Thomas Edison, probably the greatest inventor
in history, once said, "I never did a day's work in my
life. It was all fun."

He changed the lives of millions with his
inventions of the electric light and the phonograph.
He also helped perfect the motion picture, the
telephone, and the electric generator. Edison patented
more than 1100 inventions in 60 years.

What was the secret of his success? He defined it
himself as "1 percent inspiration and 99 percent
perspiration." Perhaps Edison's greatest contribution to
modern society was his attitude toward work.

Have you ever thought about the fact that God
worked? After He had completed His Creation work in

six days, He rested on the seventh. Some people think work was a condemnation upon man after Adam's sin. But work was part of Adam's life from the very beginning. God created Adam in His image and He placed man in the Garden of Eden to cultivate His creation.

Work has its rewards and laziness its consequences. The ant is a good worker. It busily gathers food for the winter without anyone giving a command. In like manner we are to initiate work ourselves and do our best. Paul reminds us not to grow weary of doing good. Work may not always be "fun," but it is essential and gives us a sense of accomplishment that nothing else can bring.

> *Now I wake me up to work,*
> *I pray thee, Lord, I will not shirk,*
> *And if You should come tonight,*
> *I pray You'll find my work's all right.*

Carrot Hearts

The good man brings good things out of the good stored up in his heart, and the evil man brings evil things out of the evil stored up in his heart. For out of the overflow of his heart his mouth speaks.

—Luke 6:45

When Peggy moved from Missouri to Idaho, she knew she needed information about gardening in the mountains.

"Your safest bet is the root crops," a native Idahoan told her. "Potatoes, beets, onions, carrots, those kind of veggies."

Taking his advice, Peggy planted her regular eight-inch carrot seeds totally unaware of the problems that lurked underground. She didn't know stones constantly pushed their way up through mountain soil. She thought her neighbors were joking when they said, "It's a great place to garden. We even grow rocks!"

When Peggy harvested her carrots, she made a disappointing discovery. Her poor carrots had pushed and twisted their way around the rocks trying with all their little carrot hearts to grow. Most of them came out of the ground looking like bright orange corkscrews.

As she tossed her curiously shaped carrots into a bucket, Pauline thought of people whose public appearance came across as just right, but who exposed their twisted hearts whenever they spoke.

She wondered, *Are my words good things that I've stored up or are they harmful? Do I encourage others and speak words of truth that I've planted in my heart through daily times in God's Word? Or, are my words destructive, coming from a critical heart?*

She quietly asked God to help her to honestly confront the harmful rocks hidden in her heart. She was willing to examine herself and make changes, but she was acutely aware of her need for God's help. On her knees in the garden was the perfect place to start.

Seasons

*Sow with a view to righteousness, reap in accordance with
kindness; break up your fallow ground, for it is time to
seek the Lord until He comes to rain righteousness on you.*
—Hosea 10:12 NASB

At a dinner party honoring Albert Einstein, a
student asked the great scientist, "What do you
actually do as a profession?" Mr. Einstein said, "I
devote myself to the study of physics." The student
then exclaimed, "You mean that you're still studying
physics? I finished mine last year."[14]

One of the very real temptations of life is to divide
it into seasons and then think of each season as an
end within itself. The student may think of the high
school diploma as the goal, and not relate it to what
he wants to do with his life. The graduate may get the
job of his choice and never consider that other jobs
could be in his future.

How often have you seen a young man and woman become engaged to be married, then spend thousands of dollars and hundreds of hours preparing for the wedding, with little or no preparation for the years of marriage ahead? Or, the couple may look forward with great anticipation to the birth of a child, with no plan for proper parenting.

The Garden of Life is a continuing cycle of seasons and years. Those who reap the greatest harvests seem to look both backward and forward. They look to the past to glean from their experiences those things that will help solve the challenges of today. They look to the future to decide which seeds they should plant today to help them attain their goals for the future.

God is present in every segment of our lives, coaxing us to learn from both our experiences and goals, that our gardens will reach their full potential.

A Mixed Bouquet of Blessing

*Every branch that does bear fruit he prunes
so that it will be even more fruitful.*
—John 15:2

Several years ago, Dale Bedford entered the karate tournament as a goal toward receiving his brown belt. But an opponent's kick in the head changed his life direction.

At first, his brain trauma was considered only minor, but the blow apparently altered his memory. Like a rose bush completely pruned back to the bare trunk, Dale was forced to start over. His ability level returned to that of a four-year-old. His math and engineering abilities disappeared, as well as his hope for a career in cable-TV engineering.

What did blossom was his artistic talent. The boy who liked to draw some girls and animals in high school and was not considered particularly "good" now supports himself with commissioned oils on canvas, earning up to $2,000 apiece. While in therapy at a rehabilitation center, Dale was required to host his own art exhibit of his work.

Dr. Eugene George, professor of neurosurgery at the University of Texas Southwestern Medical Center in Dallas, has treated hundreds of brain-injury patients. He said that it's uncommon for someone with a brain injury to develop new talents. "There are usually compensations that occur with relearning, and people with brain injuries always tend to re-evaluate what they're doing with their lives," said Dr. George.

For Dale, the accident changed the course of his life. Like a pruned bush, he did more than compensate. With appropriate training and cultivating, and the touch of the Master Gardener, a pruned bush can produce more beautiful blooms than ever.

Just ask Dale Bedford.[15]

Greener Grass?

Those who plow evil and those who sow trouble reap it.
—Job 4:8

A young man, having just finished college, landed an extremely well-paying position. He worked hard, watched others, and learned from them. He loved his wife, and his family grew. But soon he traded family time for the boardroom. He was bright and ambitious, eager to climb the corporate ladder and grasp for success. Within a few years he had risen to a top position in his company.

Suddenly others began to flock around this young wizard for professional advice—and for favors. Co-workers bribed, clients begged, and female friends flirted. The young man, eager to please and overwhelmed by the sudden attention, was blind to what was happening to him. He used his power unwisely and made some wrong financial decisions.

He neglected his family and allowed seeds of discontent to grow in his heart. From his perspective, nothing but weeds grew in his garden.

In a moment of weakness and bad judgment, the young executive fell. He succumbed to temptation, disgracing his family, quitting his job, and ultimately losing his integrity. Friends tried to help restore him, but he turned away from them. His family offered forgiveness, but the man could not forgive himself. He died a few years later, an alcoholic and a broken man.

The grass may look greener and the flowers may seem more beautiful in another garden, but there's no place like the soil where we have been planted. God knows exactly what we need. He has given us all the right ingredients for a well-watered, successful life that honors Him.

A Lifetime to Learn

Does not long life bring understanding?
—Job 12:12

Orville was nearly seventy-four years old and had been in poor health for the past ten years. Early in life he had been a robust man, working from dawn to dusk without. But now, the years had caught up with him and he tired easily—to the point that he required frequent naps throughout the day when he really felt bad. This bothered him.

He was visiting with two of his sons and reminiscing about the choices and decisions he had made throughout his life. Off and on, his voice quivered and tears welled up in his eyes as he spoke of critical times in his life where certain decisions were beneficial for the family and others had caused great hardship.

He spoke of the time he left a secure, steady job to venture into a family business. The venture did not work out and Orville and his young family struggled for years to dig out from under the mountain of debt that resulted. He also spoke of the time the family faced a mandatory move, and God guided them to the best choice of cities to relocate their home.

There were many more memories shared that afternoon. As the day wore on, the shadows lengthened in the room and Orville's eyes closed for another of his brief naps. The two sons quietly remarked to one another that the knowledge learned in a lifetime is very hard to pass on. However, they promised to learn from Dad's mistakes and to copy his successes. In short, they vowed to love life as he did, and remain faithful to family and faith as he had.

Fresh Rain

Then I will give you rain in due season,
and the land shall yield her increase.
—*Leviticus 26:4* KJV

It had been a very hot and dry month, and the wheat fields were dusty and forlorn-looking. The uncultivated plains, scattered with sagebrush and dotted by tumbleweeds, seemed to bake in the afternoon sun. The sky stretched overhead, a brassy but deep blue. What few clouds there were seemed to dangle from the sky in shapeless masses of wispy white. But when Don looked low in the sky, just above the horizon, he saw a darker line of clouds.

Eleanor stepped out the back door of her home to check on her garden. It had been so dry this summer that she had had to water three and four times a day to keep the snap beans, tomatoes, cucumbers, corn, and rhubarb from dying. As she did, she felt a hint of cooler air on her cheek. Glancing to the west, she saw that the light, wispy clouds of earlier in the day were being replaced by a growing line of towering thunderclouds heavy with much-needed rain.

As Don bounded up the walk toward the house, he couldn't help but laugh and raise his face to the gentle rain. Earlier it had been heavy, with loud thunder; now, it was a gentle, soaking rain—one that would replenish wells and nourish wheat fields. Skipping around the corner of the house, he headed for the garden to find Eleanor. Taking deep breaths, he savored the smell of a fresh prairie rain on the well-tended soil of a garden.

Sure enough, there she was, walking her garden and thanking the Father for His ever-flowing blessings.

Walking in the Garden

And they heard the sound of the Lord God walking in the garden.
—Genesis 3:8 NASB

Sleeping in was not a common occurrence for Patti growing up on a farm, not even during summer vacation from school. But Patti's mother allowed her children to sleep in once in a great while. On those rare occasions, Patti awakened gently to the smells and sounds of her mother lovingly preparing a delicious family breakfast. The aroma of sizzling bacon frying wafted through the house. Pots and pans clattered. Fresh biscuits baking in the oven provided gentle nudges to help the children shake off their slumber.

One summer morning, the house was still. Patti's brothers and sisters were sound asleep, and the kitchen was void of the usual sights and sounds and smells of meal preparation. Patti noticed that the back door was open, and she slowly eased her way out to the back porch. There she caught a glimpse of her mother weeding the garden, humming all the while. The peaceful scene wrapped itself around Patti like a cozy blanket as she watched her mother walking in the garden.

Adam and Eve lived in the only perfect garden. They could commune with nature freely, and they walked and talked with the Lord face-to-face. They heard His sounds as He walked in the garden toward them. In her spirit, Patti's mother must have known the sweetness of God's presence as she walked in her garden early in the morning. Before the demands of her day busied her hands and her mind, she wisely chose the morning quiet for a peaceful walk with God in the garden.

Forever Young

*You will be a good servant of Jesus Christ, constantly
nourished on the words of the faith and of the sound doctrine.*
—1 Timothy 4:6 NASB

General Douglas MacArthur said,

*"Whatever your years, there is in every being's
heart the love of wonder, the undaunted challenge
of events, the unfailing childlike appetite for what
is next, and the joy and the game of life. You are as
young as your faith, as old as your doubt; as
young as your self-confidence, as old as your fear;
as young as your hope, as old as your despair. In
the central place of every heart there is a recording
chamber; so long as it receives messages of beauty,
cheer, and courage, so long are you young."*

We are never too old to learn or to be used for
good. We are never too old to be awed by a thing of
beauty or to be thirsty for knowledge. Joyful living

knows no age limits, and filling our minds with delight in life may in some ways keep us forever young. Our age is not truly measured in physical characteristics and weaknesses, but by our spirit. We are always of value to our Lord. If we are willing to learn new things, develop new skills, and renew our spirits with the nourishment of God's Word, we can always grow, regardless of our age.

The growth process never really stops, even when we say we don't want to learn any more. Something inside us is always taking in something. Our choice is in whether what we're learning is helping us to grow or not.

Business as Usual?

He is not here, for He has risen, just as He said.
—*Matthew 28:6 NASB*

Along the Via Dolorosa in Jerusalem are shops with vendors touting their wares. Centuries ago, when Jesus was on His way to Calvary, He trudged along that path, notably called The Way of Suffering.

Was that day like all others? Was everything business as usual? Farmers bringing in luscious fruit and vegetables larger than you have ever seen; skinned animal meat laid bare, hanging and ready for the butcher. Noise and shouting all around; bargain hunters negotiating the prices. Dark-haired, dark-eyed boys playing in the narrow streets; Roman soldiers scurrying past black-robed Hebrews. "Just another crucifixion," a woman groans while buying a trinket. Were people too busy to even look up when Jesus made that lonely walk along the rugged cobblestones?

Business as Usual?

Amid the noise and congestion and pressing crowds, one may long for the solitude and peace of the Garden Tomb, where Jesus is believed to have been buried after the crucifixion. Amid the beauty, serenity, overhanging trees, and flowering plants, there rests a holy hush in this sacred place.

You ask me how I know He lives?
He lives within my heart!

From the Via Dolorosa to the Garden Tomb, to living within our hearts, Christ comes to us in victory over death, over sin, over the obstacles of everyday life. Nothing about his life, death, and resurrection is "business as usual." Because He is risen, the world is changed forever.

One Hundred Years!

*My job was to plant the seed in your hearts, and Apollos
watered it, but it was God, not we, who made it grow.
The ones who do the planting or watering aren't
important, but God is important because he is the
one who makes the seed grow. The one who plants and
the one who waters work as a team with the same purpose.*
—*1 Corinthians 3:6-8* NLT

*W*hile Cheryl organized her newly arrived seed
order, she found a bonus seed packet containing
cactus seeds. She flipped the envelope over to read the
planting instructions: "Seeds will germinate in one to
one hundred years."

"One hundred years!" she exclaimed aloud. "It
would take a wheelbarrow full of faith to sow those
seeds. But then, faith is what motivates most
gardeners. Few of us live to see a tree seedling grow to
its fullest potential. We cannot know if we will still be

living in the same place when our biennials bloom. Yet we plan, plant, and have faith in our work."

It's been the same for Christians since Jesus gave the "great commission" telling us to plant seeds of faith throughout the world. We are part of a team working for God. We may be the person to plant the gospel seed in someone's heart or we may be the one to water it. If faith germinates in a heart and a disciple grows, the accomplishment isn't ours but the Holy Spirit's. We may not even be around to enjoy the harvest.

Cheryl planted her cactus seeds, but they still hadn't germinated when she moved two years later. She remembered them often, however, just as she often remembered to pray for the seeds of faith she'd planted in hearts.

Thinking Things Through

You care for the land and water it; you enrich it abundantly.
The streams of God are filled with water to provide
the people with grain, for so you have ordained it.
—Psalm 65:9

One of America's most popular contemporary
painters, Andrew Wyeth, portrays life in rural
Pennsylvania and Maine so meticulously and naturally
as to sometimes appear surreal. A story told by his
brother Nat gives a great deal of insight into the
source of Wyeth's intensity:

> *Andy did a picture of Lafayette's quarters near*
> *Chadds Ford, Pennsylvania, with a sycamore tree*
> *behind the building. When I first saw the painting,*
> *he wasn't finished with it. He showed me a lot of*
> *drawings of the trunk and the sycamore's gnarled*
> *roots, and I said, "Where's all that in the picture?"*
>
> *"It's not in the picture, Nat," he said. "For me*
> *to get what I want in the part of the tree that's*

showing, I've got to know thoroughly how it is anchored in back of the house."[16]

The act of thinking things through is important to every task in our lives. We cannot overlook the importance of good preparation when we are planning our garden, or we risk damaging the plants with poor soil or by setting them too close together to grow freely.

Wall Street legend Bernard Baruch emphasized this need, stating, "Whatever failures I have known, whatever errors I have committed, whatever follies I have witnessed in private and public life have been the consequence of action without thought."

It is a joy to commune with God and ask His advice as we plan our gardens. When you have an important task to think through, take time to ask, "Lord, what is Your will?" He will be glad to help.

Share the Abundance

A generous man will himself be blessed,
for he shares his food with the poor.
—Proverbs 22:9

"A farmer whose barns were full of corn used to pray that the poor be supplied, but when anyone in need asked for corn he said he had none to spare. One day after hearing his father pray for the needy, his little son said, 'Father, I wish I had your corn.'

"'What would you do with it?' asked the father.

"The child replied, 'I would answer your prayer.'"[17]

Another child must have felt the same way. Supported by the community on Make a Difference Day, twelve-year-old Jessica Burris, her seventeen-year-old brother Jeffrey, and eleven-year-old friend Corey Woodward collected 4,500 pairs of socks and hundreds of other clothes, shoes, blankets, books, and toiletries for people seeking help at free medical clinics.

Others make a difference as well. Twelve men from the United Men of Hollandale in a Mississippi Delta farming area decided to help answer some prayers. In this area, 92 percent of people live in poverty, most jobs and stores are fifteen to twenty miles away, and there is no public transportation. These men serviced eighteen cars free for single and elderly women who were short on money.

And what about Lynda Duncan? She organized 500 volunteers in ten states. Together, they raised $4,246.78 and collected boxes of food, clothes, shoes, and toys for about 300 needy families. The Duncans gave $1,200 of their own money and delivered four 17-foot truckloads of goods to Mountain Outreach, who in turn distributed them to families in the poverty region of Appalachia.[18]

We are blessed, not so that we can tear down our barns and build bigger barns to hold our goods, but so that we can bless others with the abundance of our hearts and lives.

A Season of Love

Sons are a heritage from the Lord, children a reward from him.
—Psalm 127:3

In his book *Fatherhood,* Bill Cosby shares his humorous views on parenting. He says the poet's reason for having children is to give oneself immortality.

"We . . . did not have (children) because we thought it would be fun to see one of them sit in a chair and stick out his leg so that another one of them running by was launched like Explorer I.

"After which I said to the child who was the launching pad, 'Why did you do that?'

"'Do what?' he replied.

"'Stick out your leg.'

"'Dad, I didn't know my leg was going out. My leg, it does that a lot.'"

Cosby says, "If you cannot function in a world where things like this are said, then you better forget about raising children and go to daffodils."[19]

In fact, raising children is a lot like growing daffodils. Children, like those colorful bulbs, will bloom where they are planted. But they only bloom for a season.

Just ask Bill Cosby. In spite of his tongue-in-cheek tales about parenting, Cosby loved his son Ennis dearly but was granted only a season in which to enjoy him. An apparent robber killed Ennis in the prime of his youth.

Our children are God's gifts to us. Though they move out of our homes, they will never grow out of the garden of our hearts. Like spring daffodils, the memories of their childhood reappear continually.

Enjoy them while you can.

Holy Laughter

He will yet fill your mouth with laughter
and your lips with shouts of joy.
—Job 8:21

The air was filled with peals of laughter along with giggles of delight and chortles of joy. Just hearing it made Ron's day better. His mother had run a licensed day care facility in their home for as long as he could remember, and dozens of children from single-parent households benefited from her unconditional love. In fact, it was easy to think of their home as an oasis of love in a world lacking in it.

Ron remembered the December morning when four-year-old Louis came in from the cold and quite seriously said, "It's winter out there Reen (short for Irene)!" as he struggled to pull his arms free from his heavy coat.

Or the time when Jeffrey came by to visit and hand deliver an invitation to his high school graduation. "Grandma Reen" had cared for him throughout his elementary school years. Ron remembered Jeffrey coming from school each day of third grade. He and his best friend would exit the school with their arms draped around one another's shoulders and walk that way all the way to the car.

Many, many other memories existed. But the best, without a doubt, was that of the joyous laughter of the children as they played together. There was something so natural and carefree about the sound that anyone who heard it would know that this place was a world of safety and love—thanks to "Grandma Reen."

Have you had the chance to listen to the laughter of small children lately? Take time to listen, and your soul will be refreshed.

Flannelgraphs and Saturday Nights with Mom

*I have been reminded of your sincere faith, which first
lived in your grandmother Lois and your mother Eunice.*
—2 Timothy 1:5

Saturday evenings had a special, even magical
quality to them for young Kevin. In fact, he could hardly
wait for them to come. The routine was nearly always
the same, and it made his world safe and predictable.

First, the family would share a casual supper
together. This meal would nearly always be homemade
hamburgers, French fries, and cold pork-and-beans.
The table would include condiments for the
hamburgers, napkins for the milk mustaches, and
conversation for the heart. It was a time of love and
closeness. To this day, homemade hamburgers remind
Kevin of his childhood.

After supper, Kevin would polish everyone's Sunday dress shoes at one end of the kitchen table while at the other end, his mother prepared her Sunday school lesson for the next day.

She taught a class for young children so she used flannelgraph characters to tell the Bible stories. As she cut out the characters and rehearsed the lessons, Kevin would listen in; the stories seemed to come alive. He saw David slay Goliath, Joseph sold into slavery by his brothers, Moses leading the Israelites across the Red Sea, and many more great events so vital to the Christian heritage and faith.

It is simply amazing how much of Kevin's own faith story was learned right there as he polished shoes and listened to his mother. To this day, the smell of shoe polish brings back warm memories and bolsters his faith.

Pray for the seeds of divine truth in the fertile minds and hearts of little ones today. Pray that they will stand firm in the faith as they grow older.

Growing in Wisdom

A wise man will hear and increase in learning,
and a man of understanding will acquire wise counsel.
—Proverbs 1:5 NASB

After their wedding, the young couple prepared for their move from Ireland to America. It meant leaving their families behind and starting from scratch in a new country, but they were committed for the long haul. Even though many from their village came and settled close to them, it didn't take long for the newlyweds to realize that the man's trade would not allow him to provide for his family. What could have been the justification for a speedy retreat back to Dublin was, instead, the fuel that fired the determination to learn a new skill and prove he could provide for his family against all odds.

He and his wife agreed that Christ would be their strength and guide for the uphill battle that lay ahead. They decided that until a new skill was mastered, everything else had to take a back seat except their love and devotion to God and to each other.

The man bought a used typewriter, an adding machine, and several textbooks. After his regular job ended every day, he would sit until the wee hours of the next morning, studying, pecking away at both machines until he had taught himself how to type proficiently and how to do the work of a master accountant.

His work became so well-known that for the rest of his life he was in constant demand. It was said that his work was the finest in the land. He and his family lived very comfortable lives and he left a legacy to his children and others of a man who was willing to listen, learn, and grow in wisdom.

Righteous Fruit

And the seed whose fruit is righteousness is
sown in peace by those who make peace.
—James 3:18 NASB

*T*he role of quiet places played a very important
role in the Bible, especially in the area of faith. Christ
was alone during much of His life on earth. He would
often retreat from the multitudes for quiet reflection.
Moses went alone to the mountain to speak with God.
While there, he received the Ten Commandments, one
of the cornerstones of our faith. Daniel risked death
three times a day, when he would cease from his
labors and pray.

The Holy Spirit often speaks to us when we are alone.
Quiet places produce peace and contentment. Noise
breeds confusion. Order is often regained in silence.

Restaurants and other public places have become
so congested with noise that it makes some of these

places uncomfortable to sit in. Our culture has become so noisy with technology, industry, entertainment, and transportation, that we seldom find time and place for quiet. Yet we may yearn for times when we can think and be quiet and listen to God. Finding time—actually, *making* time—for the still times is often a daunting challenge.

If righteousness is sown in peace, then the quiet times when we just sit and listen and wait for the Lord to speak must produce what is essential for spiritual growth. Seeking quiet time for reflection helps us commune with God. As a result, His righteousness wears off on us. We begin to pick up some of His characteristics.

The Lord has time to spend with us and is ready to grow His Spirit within us. It is up to us to make the appointment.

Don't Give Up!

And let us not get tired of doing what is right,
for after a while we will reap a harvest of
blessing if we don't get discouraged and give up.
—*Galatians 6:9* TLB

With the first hint of spring, avid gardeners swoop outside, their arms loaded with seed packets. Then July shatters the gardener's enthusiasm with a hammer of one-hundred-degree temperatures. Despite the heat, endless clusters of petunias need deadheading, and quackgrass slithers across the garden.

August finds them working long hours in a hot kitchen, canning tomatoes and baking zucchini bread. When the first freeze hits in October, they hustle about the garden digging the remaining potatoes and mulching carrots.

By December, the garden is bedded down under a snowy blanket. Warm and snug inside their homes, gardeners stare out the frosty kitchen window. A contented sigh whispers through their lips as the pleasure of accomplishment seeps into their souls.

The Christian walk is similar to gardening. In the springtime of our faith, our hearts pound a rapid tempo of plans to save the world. Summer brings the discovery that our faith requires hard work. We see a need to spend long hours in God's Word to combat inaccuracies in our theology.

When we reach autumn's slower pace, in our garden of faith, we're still working but also beginning to reap the harvest. Come December, we gaze out the window of our souls with a contented, mature love of Christ. Softly exhaling the sigh of a thankful heart, we remember the joy of working with God in His perfectly planned spiritual garden.

The Worry Tree

*Therefore do not worry about tomorrow, for tomorrow will
worry about itself. Each day has enough trouble of its own.*
—Matthew 6:34

There was a man who, at the end of each work
day, would visit an old tree in his front yard before
entering his home. As he passed the tree, he would
reach out to gently touch the trunk and branches.

He did this so he could mentally "hang his
troubles" on the branches so that he would not take
them inside to his wife and children. He left his
troubles with the assumption that if the problems were
important, they would still be hanging there when he
came out the next morning. But many mornings, he
found they had disappeared.

Of course, hanging your troubles on the worry
tree is not always easy.

The Worry Tree

In his book *Still Married, Still Sober,* David Mackenzie describes another practical method for remembering to cast one's cares on God:

> To act out the principle of turning prayers over to God, we took a paper bag, wrote "God" on it, and taped it up high on the back of our kitchen door. As I prayed about matters such as my career, my role as a father, my abilities to be a good husband, I would write down each concern on a piece of paper. Then those pieces of paper would go in the bag. The rule was that if you start worrying about a matter of prayer that you've turned over to God, you have to climb up on a chair and fish it out of the bag. I don't want to admit how much time I spent sifting through those scraps of paper.[20]

Using God as your "worry tree" takes practice, but it's a skill worth developing. And your effort will be rewarded with the peace of knowing God is with you, ready to handle your heavy load—if you will let Him.

Field of Dreams

Hope deferred makes the heart sick,
but a longing fulfilled is a tree of life.
—Proverbs 13:12

There was nothing special about Randy. Each year his teachers repeated the same words: "You don't want Randy in your class. He's a loser."

But that was before he entered Miss Jewel's sixth grade art class. Until then, only bright red "D's" and "F's" adorned Randy's school papers. Test scores plummeted him to the bottom 10 percent of his class.

Miss Jewel saw the sparkle in Randy's eyes when he watched her demonstrations. His huge, rough fingers took to a paintbrush like an athlete to sports. Charcoals, sculpting, watercolor, oils—whatever the project, Randy excelled beyond any student Miss Jewel had ever seen.

She challenged him to take private lessons and suggested the names of several artists she knew. Randy made excuses for not pursuing the lessons, but Miss Jewel suspected it was because of his family's poverty.

The teacher decided to make Randy her special project. Year after year she saved her money. On Randy's graduation from high school, she sent him an anonymous check to cover his college tuition—and the name of an artist who agreed to teach Randy in the summers between his college studies.

One day about ten years later, she received a package in the mail—a beautiful oil painting of herself. And these words: "I will never forget you. I have dedicated my life to helping others grow their dreams like you did for me. Thank you, Randy."

God may give each of us a "Randy" to nurture— perhaps a child, a friend, a student, or coworker. Our words, our time, even our belief in their ability could help produce a crop of doctors, musicians, presidents, or simply loving moms or dads who will rise in their own "field of dreams."

Garden Variety Players

Now you are the body of Christ,
and each one of you is a part of it.
—1 Corinthians 12:27

For years, Daron dreamed of playing basketball. He practiced daily after school.

His dad bought a backboard and goal, and together they shot hoops in the driveway.

In his freshman year of high school, Daron failed to make the basketball team. Discouraged but refusing to quit, he kept practicing and attended all the games. He hung around after school and watched the guys practice. In his sophomore year, Daron tried out again. This time he made the team but sat on the bench most of the year. But he kept on practicing.

As a junior, Daron finally got his break and became a regular on the starting lineup. Although he could hit 75 percent of his shots, the coach rarely changed the rules: "Get the ball to Jim—as much as you can." Jim was the star of most games. He won the Most Valuable Player every year for three years and received a complete scholarship to a nearby college.

Daron expected no scholarship. After all, he was just a garden variety player. One day a coach from a prestigious university out of state called him, offering him a full scholarship.

"Why would you want me?" Daron asked.

"We've watched videos of you and your team in action, and we're impressed with your team skills. Lots of guys can be a star. But it takes a team—and a team player—to win successive games."

We may feel like "garden variety" Christians, being used in only small ways. We wonder how we could make a difference. But God is not in the business of recruiting "star" players. What He wants is a faithful heart, willing to serve Him as Heaven's team player.

The Art of Cultivation

And the secrets of his heart will be laid bare.
—1 Corinthians 14:25

"What is this, Grandpa?" asked ten-year-old Samantha.

She was exploring the contents of the garage and had come across a very strange device. It had a long handle like a rake or shovel, but on the end was a round rubber wheel with a funny attachment consisting of two interlocking circles of steel teeth. When she tried to roll it on the concrete floor, the steel teeth prevented the rubber wheel from touching the floor and it made an awful racket.

Turning from his workbench, Grandpa Bill smiled. "Sweetheart, that is a cultivator, and it is used in our garden. Those teeth break up the surface of the soil and uproot weeds. Breaking up the soil allows water and nutrients to get to the roots of our vegetables, and getting rid of the weeds allows them to grow freely."

"Wow, Grandpa, that's neat. Our Sunday school teacher was telling us the story of how a man's enemy put bad seeds in his wheat and then weeds grew up.[21] If they would have had a cultivator like this, they could have removed the weeds without waiting until the harvest."

"Yes, you are right," Bill replied. "The hard soil and weeds in my life need cultivating, too. When something is not good for me, I have to clean those 'spiritual weeds' out of my life."

"I never thought of it that way before, Grandpa. When I do wrong and then I feel bad, is God just getting my attention now so I can do it better next time?"

"Yes," Grandpa Bill replied. "He uproots the bad weeds in our hearts, and breaks up the soil so He can plant good things."

Friday Night Bravery

So we say with confidence,
'The Lord is my helper; I will not be afraid.'
—Hebrews 13:6

He was a really skinny, little kid even though he was a junior in high school. And to his younger brother, it was unbelievable how loud Don wheezed when his asthma struck in full force. About once a month, Bobby would be awakened by the sound of Don gasping for breath. Just as soon as he could suck in air, Don would be shaking and gasping for the next breath. Sometimes their parents would rush Don to the emergency room for treatment.

The doctors said that it was the hot, sticky atmosphere or perhaps the smog of the downtown streets that triggered the attacks. They advised Don to stay indoors during the summer months when the humidity was highest. The doctors said that if he stayed indoors, he might be spared from the worst of his asthma attacks.

The problem was that Don and his church youth group had a standing commitment to conduct street revival services every Friday evening, and Don was usually the one to preach. He was determined to never miss an opportunity to fulfill his life calling. So, he continued to preach, no matter the weather, and every once in a while he would fight off the asthma attacks. He counted the cost and decided to take the risk.

More than thirty years later, Don is a seasoned missionary in South America. His dedication to sharing the Good News continues to provide inspiration for others. And, he still never misses an opportunity to preach. For his brother, Don's Friday night bravery remains a source of encouragement as he, too, grows in his faith.

Nothing Is Impossible with God

I can do all things through Him who strengthens me.
—Philippians 4:13 NASB

Scientists say it can't be done! It's impossible. Aerodynamic theory is crystal clear. Bumblebees cannot fly.

The reason is because the size, weight, and shape of the bumblebee's body in relation to the total wing spread makes it impossible to fly. The bumblebee is simply too heavy, too wide, and too large to fly with wings that small.

However, the bumblebee is ignorant of these scientific facts and goes ahead and flies anyway.

It was God who created the bumblebee and God who taught him how to fly. The bumblebee obviously didn't question God about the problem with aerodynamics. He simply flew. He didn't question whether God really knew what He was talking about. He simply flew. He didn't wonder if God really loved him when He gave him such small wings. He simply flew.

When God created us, He also equipped us for the life ahead. He says He knows the plans He has for our lives. Because He loves us, He has promised to be with us, to teach us, to carry us, to be our rock. All we have to do is trust and obey.

God is not limited by our understanding of how things happen. Just because we can't see something, doesn't mean it's not real. Faith is, indeed, the substance of things not seen. Sometimes life is unexplainable, and the impossible happens. We can't always explain everything.

And just because we don't understand how something can be done, doesn't mean Almighty God can't do it.

Freedom to Dance

It is for freedom that Christ has set us free.
Stand firm, then, and do not let yourselves be
burdened again by a yoke of slavery.
—*Galatians 5:1*

As a child, Ellen loved her Uncle Merrill's garden. The plants that captured her attention most were the hundreds of white gladioli planted in long, straight rows just like Uncle Merrill's sweet corn. It frustrated Ellen, however, when a breeze forced the tall, slender flowers to sway out of position. She preferred to see them standing tall and erect instead of dancing in the breeze.

As Ellen grew into adulthood, she tried to make her life perfect like Uncle Merrill's rows of sweet corn instead of his gladioli. She tried with all her might to march a narrow, straight line, but she constantly swayed out of the rigid position.

One day in utter frustration, she cried out to God, "I can't do it! These rules are too heavy a burden." After a good cry, she decided to go see Uncle Merrill.

Ellen sat in her car a long time watching Uncle Merrill's white gladioli weave back and forth in the breeze. Slowly she began to see that although the flowers freely danced in the sunshine, they remained firmly rooted in the soil. Those stalks of glorious white blossoms proclaimed to her a joyous message. If her heart is firmly rooted in Christ, she is free to rejoice in her faith. When Ellen attempted to abide by a lengthy list of harsh rules, she realized she was choosing slavery when God had already set her free.

Finally, she understood that God's yoke of love is gentle, and His burden is light. Like the gladioli, she could dance freely in a summer breeze.

Silver Petals: Young or Old?

*Remember your Creator in the days of your
youth before the . . . silver cord is severed . . .
and the spirit returns to God who gave it.*
—Ecclesiastes 12:1, 6-7

A dozen children and adults were quizzed on a television program: "What is the best age of life to be alive?"

"Two months, because you would be carried around. And you had lots of love and care."

"Three years, because you didn't have to go to school. You could do pretty much what you wanted, and could play most of the time."

"Eighteen. Because you are out of high school and you can drive in New York City."

"Twenty-five. Because you have more pep."

A three-year-old girl said, "the best age to be alive was twenty-nine, because at that age you could lie around the house, sleep, and loaf most of the time."

"Forty, because you are in the prime of life and vitality."

"Fifty-five because you are over your responsibilities of raising your children and can enjoy life and grandchildren."

"Sixty-five, because after that you can enjoy retirement."

The last person, an elderly woman, commented, "all ages are good, so enjoy the age you are now."[22]

If we present our lives to God while we are young, like a silvery, petaled rose, we have much to offer Him—and much to enjoy. But if we were to pluck one petal from that rose for every few years we delay, by the time we reached our December years, we would have nothing but a bare stem to offer God—and very little time to enjoy.

The best age to be alive is now—but the best time to surrender to God is while we are young.

In the Winter of My Heart

The winter is past; the rains are over
and gone…the season of singing has come.
—Song of Songs 2:11-12

It was already winter in the Szuber family,
even though autumn's leaves had not yet fallen. They
were grieving.

When the car Patti Szuber was riding in hit a rock
wall in Knoxville, Tennessee, and careened onto the
road, rolling several times, the twenty-two-year-old
beauty was killed.

Patti was an organ donor, and her family could
choose who would be the recipient of her heart—an
unknown person on the national waiting list or
someone they knew. On the national list, in slot
#2,935, was Chester Szuber, Patti's father. He had
undergone three open-heart surgeries and two
angioplasties and lived with life-threatening heartbeat

irregularities. Since his health was so serious, there were no real guarantees that Patti's heart would help Mr. Szuber. But he was willing: "It would be a joy to have Patti's heart."

Five hours and fifty-one minutes after Patti's heart stopped beating in Tennessee, it was functioning well in her father's chest. The transplant was successful.[23]

Winter, like the difficult season in the Szuber family, comes almost brutally at times, it seems. Nature, once vibrant with color and energy, sheds its life, leaving only bare branches—like bare hearts exposed. But God in His wisdom and divine plan knows that without death there can be no life. Seeds, just like His own Son, once dying, soon spring forth in another "body," breathing life and hope and second chances.

Those who understand this principle will find a true home in the Father's heart.

Roofing Hammer

His God instructs him and teaches him the right way.
—Isaiah 28:26

The three young men were working on the roof of granddad's house all morning. The day before, David had removed all of the old shingles and had put down the new tarpaper. Now, they were putting the new roof on, and it was a lot of work. First, they finished the roof of the front porch. That entailed carrying three heavy rolls of roofing up the ladder, cutting them to size, and nailing them down. Next came the regular shingles.

As the morning went along, Randy became frustrated because it was taking him a long time to be sure that each shingle was positioned correctly. It seemed that no matter how hard he tried, he had to reposition it several times.

Finally, David brought Randy a roofing hammer to use. It was a funny-looking hammer with a little nob on one side. "If you don't mind let me show you how to use this hammer to position the shingle." With that, he demonstrated for the use of the small knob. It was a measurement guide, and when used correctly, you could align the shingle in a matter of seconds. Once Randy got the hang of it, it was amazing how much quicker he was able to position the shingles.

Thank goodness, I finally know the right way to do this, Randy thought.

Successful Christian living is much like roofing. If you learn how to use the tools (prayer, worship, and study of the Word) correctly, then your ability to finish the job is enhanced. Just as Randy had to listen to David to learn the correct way to use the hammer, we must learn to listen to God to learn the correct way to succeed for Him.

Planting for a Lifetime

You are the light of the world.
—*Matthew 5:14*

Eight-year-old Ray looked with open adoration and love at his pastor. He was an unremarkable man in many ways—small and thin with a wisp of hair on top of his head. To Ray though, Pastor Majors was right next to God in holiness. He was gentle, with a kind, loving heart. With his eyes closed, Pastor Majors played hymns on his harmonica.

Pastor Majors could recite any verse in the entire Bible. God had blessed him with a "photographic memory" of the Holy Scripture. He never read aloud from the Bible; he only recited it. One Sunday evening he shared a story from his own youth that planted seeds of faith and courage in Ray's heart—seeds that would take root and stay with him for a lifetime.

"I was in high school when I broke my neck," the pastor said. "I was on the top of a school bus packing the band instruments to leave on a trip when I fell off and landed on my head. It was my faith in God that allowed me to recover and play music again."

The story impacted Ray's life deeply. We never know when what we say will have a life-lasting impact. For Ray, his pastor's story of faith as a teenager helped Ray grow faith in his own heart over the course of his lifetime.

Henry George said, "Let no man imagine that he has no influence."[24] We cannot stop our influence; but we can choose which types of seeds we will plant.

The Birthday

The righteous shall flourish.
—*Psalm 92:12* KJV

Eleven-year-old Will hurried ahead of the rest of the party as they arrived at the restaurant for dinner to celebrate his mother's birthday. When everyone else came through the door, he had already spoken to the hostess informing her that they would need a table for a party of seven in the nonsmoking section. The table was waiting and the group quickly seated. Throughout the dinner, Will, seated between his two grandfathers, was engaging and polite. He and his grandfathers seemed to share a secret as they whispered to each other off and on during dinner. He smiled often at his mother and winked knowingly.

Finally, as dinner came to a conclusion, the waiter arrived at the table with a beautifully presented and delicious serving of cheesecake topped with fresh berries. The dessert was for Will's mother for her birthday. Coffee cups were refilled and fresh forks provided as Will's mother shared the wonderful dessert with her family. Will, grinning, giggling, and outright laughing, clapped his hands and said, "Now you know why I was winking, don't ya, Mom!"

Later Will's parents commented on what a delightful young man he was becoming. It hardly seemed possible that this was the same little boy who just a few short years earlier had been so shy and withdrawn that you could barely get him to say hello to a waiter. Now, he was making arrangements for the entire dinner party.

Spiritual growth is just like that too. When we surround ourselves with other believers, study His Word, attend worship, and pray faithfully, we cannot help but grow in the Lord. And as we grow in Christ, we naturally become a blessing to others and serve as a spirit of encouragement.

Corn on the Cob

The pastures are clothed with flocks;
the valleys also are covered over with corn.
—Psalm 65:13 KJV

*B*utter dripped from the fresh corn on the cob.
It was amazing how black the grains of pepper were
against the bright yellow kernels. These ears of corn
had come directly from Aunt Elsie's backyard garden
and were without a doubt the sweetest corn Bobby
ever tasted. He was going to enjoy every bite. It didn't
matter if the butter dripped off onto his jeans or that
he had to wipe juice from his chin with the back of
his hand. He had been looking forward to this meal all
the way from Texas to Colorado.

Bobby's family always went to Colorado each
summer. The trip would take nearly twenty-four
hours, and as soon as the car stopped in Aunt Elsie
and Uncle Denny's driveway, Bobby would race to the
backyard to see her corn. Without fail, there it would

stand; row upon row of beautiful, green corn plants loaded with ears ripe for the picking. He enjoyed walking between the rows as the plants towered over him with the blue sky above and the moist earth cool to the touch of his bare feet. Then, Aunt Elsie would come out and show him which ears to pick for supper.

Finally, supper would be ready. Uncle Denny would have come in from work by then, and once the family had gathered around the table, he would give thanks. No matter what he prayed, Bobby would always add special thanks for the corn.

All around us are sweet blessings from heaven—ordinary, daily things for some may bring endless delight to others. A simple ear of corn brought endless joy to Bobby year after year. Like Bobby, we can savor our blessings and give thanks.

References

Unless otherwise indicated, all scripture quotations are taken from the *Holy Bible, New International Version*®. NIV®. Copyright © 1973, 1978, 1984, by International Bible Society. Used by permissions of Zondervan Publishing House. All rights reserved.

Verses marked TLB are take from *The Living Bible* © 1971. Used by permission of Tyndale House Publishers, Inc., Wheaton, Illinois 60189. All rights reserved.

Scriptures marked NCV are quoted from *The Holy Bible, New Century Version*, © 1978, 1988, 1991, by Word Publishing, Dallas, Texas 75039. Used by Permission.

Scripture quotations marked KJV are taken from the *King James Version* of the Bible.

Scripture quotations marked NASB are taken from the *New American Standard Bible*. Copyright © The Lockman Foundation 1960, 1962, 1968, 1971, 1972, 1973, 1975, 1977. Used by permission.

Scripture quotations marked AMP are taken from *The Amplified Bible New Testament*. Copyright © 1958, 1987 by the Lockman Foundation, La Habra, California, used by permission.

Scripture quotations marked THE MESSAGE are taken from *The Message*. Copyright © 1993, 1994, 1995. Used by permission of NavPress Publishing Group.

Scripture quotations marked RSV are taken from *The Revised Standard Version of the Bible*, Copyright © 1946, Old Testament section copyright © 1952 by the Division of Christian Education of the Churches of Christ in the United States of America and is used by permission.

Scripture quotations marked NLT are taken from the *Holy Bible, New Living Translation*, copyright © 1996. Used by permission of Tyndale House Publishers, Inc., Wheaton, Illinois 60189. All rights reserved.

Endnotes

[1] Maugham, W. Somerset. *Of Human Bondage,* Doubleday, Garden City, New York, 1936.

[2] Chorus by Mary Maxwell, Score by Ada Rose Gibbs.

[3] *Today in the Word* May 1990, MBI.

[4] Wilson, Marvin R., *Our Father Abraham: Jewish Roots of the Christian Faith,* Wm. B. Eerdmans Publishing Company, Grand Rapids, Michigan, 1989.

[5] Swindoll, Charles R., *Seasons of Life,* Multnomah Press, Portland Oregon, 1983.

[6] Meier, Paul, M.D., "Confessions of a Workaholic," *The Physician,* March/April 1990.

[7] Sweeting, George, *Who Said That?* Moody Press, Chicago, Illinois, 1995.

[8] Cymbala, Jim with Merrill, Dean, *Fresh Wind, Fresh Fire,* Zondervan Publishing House, Grand Rapids, Michigan 1997.

[9] "Opportunities Missed," Author Unknown.

[10] Monty, Shirley, *May's Boy,* Thomas Nelson Publishers, 1981.

[11] Swindoll, Charles R., *Seasons of Life,* Multnomah Press, Portland Oregon, 1983.

[12] Sweeting, George, *Who Said That?* Moody Press, Chicago, Illinois, 1995.

[13] Seager, Jynnette, "A Country Garden Fair" *Virtue,* June/July 1999.

[14] *Today in the Word,* September 25, 1992.

[15] Dickinson, Joy, "A Mixed Blessing," *The Dallas Morning News,* January 10, 1999.

[16] *Inventors at Work: Interviews with 16 Notable American Inventors,* Kenneth A. Brown.

[17] Flynn, Leslie B., *Come Alive with Illustrations,* Baker Book House, Grand Rapids, Michigan, 1988.

[18] Greenville Herald Banner, *USA Weekend,* April 19, 1996.

[19] Cosby, Bill, *Fatherhood,* Berkley Books, New York, 1986.

[20] David Mackenzie, *Still Married, Still Sober,* IVP, 1991, p. 117.

[21] Parable of the Tares, Matthew 13:24-30.

[22] Flynn, Leslie B., *Come Alive with Illustrations,* Baker Book House, Grand Rapids, Michigan, 1988.

[23] Loven, Jennifer, *Dallas Morning News,* August 26, 1994.

[24] Sweeting, George, *Who Said That?* Moody Press, Chicago, Illinois, 1995.

Additional copies of this book and other titles
in the *Quiet Moments with God Devotional* series
are available at your local bookstore.

Clothbound devotionals:
Breakfast with God
Coffee Break with God
Sunset with God
Tea Time with God
Daybreak with God
Through the Night with God
In the Kitchen with God

Portable gift editions:
Breakfast with God
Coffee Break with God
Sunset with God
Tea Time with God

If you have enjoyed this book, or if it has
impacted your life, we would like to hear from you.
Please contact us at:

Honor Books
Department E
P.O. Box 55388
Tulsa, Oklahoma 74155